GIVING UP

The Memoir of a Quitter

Hey New Friend!

Abigail here! I dropped this book knowing that it would find you at the Perfect time. May it reach & unleash your Heart!

Let me know you found it by tagging me on insta @_instagail_

Abigail Gazda

Enjoy! *Abigail*

abigailgazda.com

PINA PUBLISHING 🍍 SEATTLE

The stories and events that appear in this book are true.

Text copyright © 2017 by Abigail Gazda
Cover design by Emily Gazda © 2017 by Abigail Gazda
Cover photo by Lindsey Williams © 2017 by Abigail Gazda
Interior book design by Susan Harring © 2017 by Pina Publishing

For information about special discounts for bulk purchases contact:
sales@pinapublishing.com

Manufactured in the United States of America
Library of Congress Cataloging-in-Publication Data Gazda, Abigail.

Summary:
Giving Up Giving Up: The Memoir of a Quitter is a self-help book in the form of a memoir, by author Abigail Gazda. The intention of this four-part book is to have readers take a look at how their life has come to be. Through personal anecdotes and powerful questioning, Abigail will guide you to clear the space to unleash your greatness. Gazda, who's made her own "hot mess" of transformation, invites you to get your hands dirty digging into this book, and beginning your journey of stepping into your power. With a history of ontological training in her back pocket, Abigail shares her own breakdowns, breakthroughs, and possibilities, in order to empower readers to accept themselves and create a life they love.

ISBN: 978-1-943493-17-3 (softcover)
ISBN: 978-1-943493-21-0 (e-book)

[Memoir-Nonfiction. Self-Help-Nonfiction. Ontological Coaching.
Transformation. Empowerment.]

The dedication of this book is in loving memory of
Samantha Ann Plavec:

My dearest Samantha,
you have been frozen in time, my love.

Your life was halted at its peak.
The Universe stopped you dead in your tracks, to live
forever as a shining example of courage, adventure,
joy, and commitment to a full life.

Your untimely departure will not go unappreciated or
understated. You have become a beautiful gift to every
human in your life still stretching their arms for
what can be their greatest adventure!

Thank you for keeping us laughing.
Thank you for keeping us smiling.
This world would never have been
the same without you.
I, personally, would have never been
the same without you.

You are a trailblazer
and this is just another trail you've blazed.
I absolutely love you.
Thank you for being a gift in your time, and beyond.
I promise with everything I have
to live by the lesson you've taught:
to cherish everything,
and everyone,
and every day.

Rest assured, Sam.
You left us with your love.

Table of Contents

Preface

"So where did you learn how to quit?" my inner child specialist, Kathy, asked me as I sobbed in a virtual internet therapy session. I sat silently perplexed about how far back my quitting went. How deeply rooted was my natural born Runner?

"Well, I guess I learned it from my parent's divorce," I answered clumsily. It seemed like the most obvious answer at the moment, and I watched her shake her head in agreement as though she already assumed that to be true. After some contemplation, I then briefed her that I wasn't so sure that was the case, considering my parents got divorced when I was two. In retrospect, it seemed unlikely that they would be the origin of this phenomenon, as I had never even seen them hug or kiss.

Upon completion of the session, and in the following days, I pondered her questions. I got to digging deeper into my heart and memories. I sent her a follow-up email discussing the thoughts I had been sifting through. After further reflection, I had decided that I learned to quit as an adult because I was never allowed to quit as a child. In my youth, I was made to 'tough it out.' I was conditioned to believe that quitting was for the weak-minded. I had come to believe that quitting was a black mark at the pearly gates. Only losers quit. 'Quitters never win,' you already know the song and dance, I'm sure.

At the age of twenty-seven, I found myself doing everything possible to solve the problem of being me. I was doing everything imaginable, from hiring an inner child specialist to joining a support group for divorcees, to find out what was so wrong with me that caused my life to arrive at this point. I was broken all the way down and had no idea how to build myself back up. I was constantly hurting, and I was constantly trying to find and fix the broken part of me.

Over the course of my transformation, I have come to know myself in a more realistic way. As I plunged into self-development, the more I looked, the more I found. I began to see some obvious patterns playing out in my life. While the circumstances of my life changed, my patterns proved to be constant. Seeing them in retrospect demonstrated a recipe for disaster. Seeing these patterns evident at every phase of life had me putting all the ingredients together to see how I had created this smorgasbord of grudges, misunderstandings, disappointments, and pitfalls. Spending a year reflecting on the stages of my life led me to peeling back new layers of my onion. As I have healed and peeled and chopped and slow simmered, I have always evolved. This seemingly endless pursuit has resulted in my seeing the core of who I am.

As you can expect, peeling back onions can cause tears and quite a mess. Your hands smell the whole rest of the day and so does the kitchen. But the more cooking I did, I noticed myself becoming a more fully developed, fully empowered, fully expressed, and fully flavorful woman.

Ultimately, my recipes have come out pretty well—tasty and enjoyed by many. A few came out too salty. A few went straight from the pan to the trash. For the most part, I would consider myself a pretty good cook, which my Slovak ancestors would surely be proud of.

As I share my evolution and transformation with you, I welcome you to enjoy my story, but really, I invite you to apply my recipe with your own ingredients. Explore the depths of your heart and begin to peel back the layers of your own onion. You will find reflection questions at the end of several chapters. The names, dates, and places in this book are mine, but the transformation will be yours. I invite you to reflect by taking a 'look in the mirror,' and see how you relate in your own life. This book is an opportunity to discover possibilities in yourself, and take a step in creating your life powerfully. I acknowledge you for picking up this book.

Reflection Questions:

Do you consider yourself a quitter?

Have you been known to 'stick-with-it' in situations you'd rather leave?

What is the relationship you have with commitment?

Would it be like you to quit reading this book about now?

Part One

Never Quitting

Chapter 1

Winners Never Quit

My first memory of not being allowed to quit is middle school band. Cue the trumpets! It is the story that sits the deepest in my non-quitting chamber. I can still tell the story with as much emotion as fourteen-year-old me, and I can feel myself reverting back to her as I take myself into my deepest memory banks to write this. I can vividly recall the five-year commitment to practices, summer sessions, parade marching, and nerve-racking spring performances.

The band director would come to the third-grade classroom each spring to entice us wild ones with a variety of instruments on display when we got back from recess. With all the shiny things lined up, we were given the chance to try out as many as we wanted. Being the tomboy that I was, I wanted to play the trumpet. It seemed the coolest, but I couldn't make that damn buzzing noise with my lips. So, trumpet was off the list, and that also wiped out trombone for my second place option—and a quarter of the instruments for that matter. By the end of the selection process, I went with the saxophone, just because it wasn't the clarinet.

I also chose the saxophone because a boy I had a crush on chose it as well. He was super cool, outgoing, and cute. We would joke around and doodle on our music sheets. We would giggle behind our music stands every time we got the evil eye for goofing off between songs. I would daydream about him falling in love with me, so band was really cool—for about the first year.

It was all fun and flirting until the day I got braces. Playing the saxophone became as pleasant as ripping open stitches and having to get new stitches in your mouth…every day.

So, I wanted to quit.

I kept it a secret for a long time because I was embarrassed about the idea of wanting to quit anything. I remember complaining about my mouth in hopes to get my mom in agreement that it would be 'okay' to quit. I mean, my pearly whites were at risk! I thought getting off the hook was a shoo-in.

Did I mention earlier that winners never quit?

I got wax to cover my train tracks, and back to band practice I was sent. It was *super* cute. I looked like a hockey player rocking mouth wax—and I had an interesting new speech impediment. It was a convenient band-aid fix for my surface problem, but I still had a quitting problem. By the end of the year, I had developed a communication problem as well. I was left feeling misunderstood as well as frustrated with myself for not sharing what I truly wanted: to be allowed to quit band guilt-free.

As we aged into middle school, other kids' parents let them quit. My band mates were disappearing by the week! I would come to Monday practice with my own wagers for who wouldn't be there next. I was bummed. I felt left behind to suffer. It was the end of everything when the boy I had a crush on got to quit. I was so envious.

So here I was, in a band I didn't want to be in, with bleeding gums and no boy to distract me from it. Game over. I was officially checked out but still showing up to go through the motions for a full year. It was sixth grade, I felt like a "band nerd," and I was pretty resentful about it, too.

Then, something happened. In seventh grade, I came to terms with the fact that the only way out of band was completing it as a graduating eighth grader. I accepted this fate, and I decided that I was officially "in it to win it." I decided that if I wasn't allowed to quit, then I would be the single best non-quitter there ever was! I took on leadership. I took on practicing and becoming first chair. I took on perfecting what was expected of me and being the bomb-diggity in band. So I did, and so I was. Abigail the Achiever began to take shape and formulate an equation to dominate challenges and adversity.

Chapter 2

The Rest of It

To condense the rest of story about not quitting in my childhood: I was a girl scout until the eighth grade. I played three sports year-round in high school. I was president of my class. I graduated with honors. I graduated Sigma Cum Laude. I was Senior of the Year at my college. I took on perfection as a way of being and began to place my value in a list of accomplishments on my college applications and resumes. I wanted to win everything and take the lead everywhere.

I became somewhat obsessed with awards, certificates, and certifications that would represent my qualification for, and ultimate worthiness of love and affection. It wasn't until becoming a life coach that I came to understand the way of being I had constructed in my childhood. I had learned early on that quitters are frowned upon, so I decided I would be anything but a quitter.

My middle school brain understood all the negativity and guilt cast on quitters, and I had already opted out of that. I didn't want to put myself at risk for rejection as a quitter or someone who didn't follow through, so I chose the *way other side* of the spectrum. I created a winning strategy that set me up working really hard and forcing outcomes. I had generated the equation: work hard in order to achieve and impress, in order to gain recognition, in order to feel loved. You can see how many times I used "in order to," because that was how I had computed conditions of love. Being the very best at everything was the only access I had at the time to feeling lovable and worthy. Acceptance and affinity couldn't just be present in my life. It must be earned. So, I earned it. Hard.

Chapter 3

"But I Don't Know How to Quit!"

"Well then, Abby! Why don't you just quit!?" my mom shouted at me as I had a full-blown panic attack in the back seat over going back to college basketball after winter break. As a college athlete, every year we got three days home for Christmas, and my days home were few and far between. The impending doom that the holiday joy was coming to its dreary end sent me spiraling head first into hyperventilation. My sister sat silently in the front seat and I, with my head tucked between my knees, was panting and sobbing in the back.

It made me cry even harder to finally have permission to quit from the woman that held me accountable my entire life. It was the biggest WHAT-THE-HELL moment I had ever experienced. I spent my whole life *not quitting* in order to please, and *now* I was getting agreement that it was okay to quit something when the fact of the matter was, I didn't know how. I had actually become so conditioned to stick it out that quitting wasn't a real option. I had no idea what it would really look like to walk away from anything. Based on what I had heard about quitters throughout my whole life, quitting certainly wasn't desirable or awe-inspiring.

So here I am. A twenty-two-year-old over-achieving perfectionist, who measured love in medals and certificates, being told that it was actually making me quite the little monster. The sad part was that I knew no other way to be. I only knew how to achieve. It was the only access I had to feeling lovable and worthy, and I wasn't ready to give that up.

College ball really tipped the scale for me because, not only was I far too short and slow, blowing out my knee my sophomore year should have been the end of my jersey days. But, it wasn't. I didn't know how to quit. I forged on the only way I knew how: relentlessly. I attempted to play two years longer than I should have, and it showed. I lost my captainship, my patience, my self-worth and self-love. I became very disconnected from the present, wishing myself into the past or the future—anywhere but where I was.

The identities of my inner critic began to develop power in those years. The internal dialogue I wrestled with was a conversation about never being good enough. I was not tall, fast, smart, quick, or strong enough to be a college basketball player. Blowing out my knee cast a spotlight on all of the shortcomings that I was compensating for with my work ethic. The jig was up on my strategy to make it in college ball. I was angry and resentful. I had a grudge about my ACL tear. I was seriously struggling through this battle, but damn was I committed! I thought not quitting counted for something about my character. What was really happening was that I could not face the reality that it was not beneficial for my mental or physical health to continue with basketball. I could not see, at this age, that my commitment to basketball was fulfilled in high school. It was further fulfilled having completed a year of college ball. I made it. I achieved my dream.

Tearing my ACL and struggling through three long years of a painful injury-recovery-injury-recovery cycle was evidence for the reality that letting go was a concept that I simply could not grasp. I believe the layman's term for this is 'hard-headed.' I couldn't put the pieces together about how years of commitment didn't have a happier ending. I couldn't walk away feeling like I failed, so I didn't walk away. I dragged my feet, and face, through the mud of what I thought it meant to be committed. So, of course, trying to make it to the end of my senior season was a nightmare, not just for me, but everyone involved. I couldn't even see it for what it was.

Now that I have sufficiently mucked up the energy here, please allow me to begin cleaning it up. This isn't an entire book about my woes. It is a chance to look and see that the foundation you have seemingly built your life on is malleable. It is something that can be fundamentally transformed in such a way that you can recreate who you believe yourself to be.

Something to consider, is that you are where you are because it is as far as you believe you can go. Even if you still hold onto your dreams, you have written them off as only dreams. Whenever we consider taking a step further into our dream lives, we allow the voice in our head to talk us off the ledge of our bravery. I like to call that voice our 'inner critic.' Its only job is to keep us safe, comfortable, and looking good to others. The chatter which this inner voice creates has nothing to do with our dream lives, and everything to do with our human desire for ensured safety. When this occurs in such a way that we do in fact surrender our dreams, I like to refer to this phenomenon as *taking what you can get, as opposed to going for what you want.* We never really surrender our desires; we relinquish the will and power to go outside of our comfort zones to attain them. As we age, those dreams simply become the things we never got to do because 'life happened to us.'

All I knew through age twenty-three was relentless commitment. I thought holding onto basketball was part of my dream. I could not understand that I fulfilled my goal as a freshman by making it onto a college team. As a non-quitter, I had to take my basketball career as far as I could. My relentlessness got me as far as it could before spontaneously combusting in my face…or in my knee. I thought work ethic was the answer. I had a limited number of tools to deal with, cope with, and create life powerfully. This became more obvious as I grew older. I could see that something had to shift. Staying where I was on the maturity spectrum would have cost me the rest of my life, and many of my dreams.

Reflection Questions:

Are you dragging your feet through the mud of an undesired commitment just to stay comfortable, safe, or look good to others?

Where in your life are you refusing to quit something that is causing your perceived misery?

What are you struggling to let go of in that commitment?

What are you getting out of staying?

There *is* a difference between quitting something after having fulfilled a commitment and just being done. I fulfilled my dream of being a college athlete by becoming one. It did not require my further injuring myself to remain one. When in life have you fulfilled a commitment, but are now stringing it along further than was your original intent?

Part Two

Quitting Everything

Chapter 1

The Subtle Quitter

"Well, I was baptized Roman Catholic, but I'm not practicing. I would just consider myself spiritual."

I'm willing to bet those of us raised in a religion have made some version of this concession at one point or another in our lives. We were raised with stories and parables of right and wrong, Heaven and Hell, and all or nothing. We were conditioned to believe that the rules of man equated to the rules of the Universe. Religions were created to generate structure, identity, and conformity aligned with a belief system. They have shaped lives, generations, cultures, and eras.

I must say, I quit religion very slowly. I had always struggled with the name 'God.' I had related to Jesus as a parable character—nothin' personal, Jesus. I had never really quit religion publicly because I was too scared of eternal damnation. For a large portion of my life, I feared *they* might be right. What if I screwed around about religion my whole life and ended up in Hell? So, I skirted around this concern by showing up for mass on Christmas and Easter. My kind is fondly referred to as a 'Chreaster' in the Catholic community.

From a very young age, church was built into my education. Mass was part of the Tuesday/Thursday school routine. In eighth grade, I used to feel obligated to go to mass because we had weekly assignments to summarize the homily (what the priest said about the Gospel) to prove we went. That was the maximum level of my commitment to my religion. I related to it as a class, rather than a belief system. I knew what was expected of me as a Catholic—after all, there are ten major rules—but I never really connected to it as a way of being. Instead, I just went through the motions of obedience that were expected of me.

The Subtle Quitter was exactly that, subtle. She was so subtle, in fact, that I didn't know she existed in my younger years. She was sly and attempted to be discreet. This quitter wanted everyone to think she was committed, while trying to get away without committing to anything. She tried to be the one sneaking out the back door while no one was paying attention. This version of me played along with what others thought was best, but silently doubted and resented them for having an opinion about how I should live my life.

Going to a public high school was the perfect excuse to slowly lose my religion. No one made me go and no one kept track of me. I would get the occasional 'Catholic Guilt Trip' with a 'we miss you at church!' but I always knew it was from a place of obligation, not necessarily concern or compassion. Overall, I thought I was going to get away with quitting my religion unnoticed. Then, I found Christianity. My new sweet and spunky high school best friend introduced it to me. She invited me to her church freshman year, and it immediately felt different. They sang, clapped, and even danced during the service! Their services were more current, and we didn't have to kneel, ever. I was all about singing for Jesus, so it became fun. It became relatable. It became a place that I fit into comfortably, so I went with it. Throughout high school this was my jam, along with sports and school.

This was the time in my life that I actually became aware of the Subtle Quitter. I found this new church as a way out of my old one. I was beginning to accept to myself that I didn't believe in Catholicism. I thought it would fly that if I wasn't going to Catholic church, at least I was going to a church.

It wasn't until later in life that I found out how much backlash my mom was protecting me from.

As I look back on it, I can't say I was anymore connected to God and Jesus while attending my new church, but I did feel a sense of belonging. I began to feel connected to the unity I felt within its walls. It was a milestone in the journey of finding my faith.

After four years of singin', swingin', and swayin', I went to a Catholic college. Praise Jesus nobody tracked my spiritual journey here! I related to college as an opportunity to play basketball and stumble home to my dorm room after a night of drinking without a guilt trip or getting grounded for the week. I must admit, church was the very last thing on my mind.

My sophomore year, I found Kairos. It is a religious retreat that our school hosted, in which I began to discover the authentic leadership role within me. I went as an attendee and was immediately seen as a leader. I inspired conversation. I supported peers and led groups. At the end of the retreat, they had us do a funny little exercise in which we wrote a letter to ourselves as God. This was the very first time I felt a true presence from within and without. I still played along with all this 'God' talk, but I found myself simply writing to myself with complete love, acceptance, and kindness.

I received that letter in the mail sometime later and remembered every word. I remember the timelessness of it. Loving yourself never gets old, but I realized how quickly it can slip away. Loving yourself takes a conscious effort that I wasn't willing to put forth consistently at the time. That letter reminded me of my love for myself, and I recalled my love and leadership from the retreat. That letter called me to become a living example of love in the world. I was inspired to be a light for others, but I still wasn't sure about giving God the credit.

I was invited back as a leader for the next Kairos retreat and spoke to the whole group as though I was reading from the Gospel of Gazda. I was speaking straight from my heart—leading straight from my heart, as I was sharing my heart with others. I can say that it only occurred to me when writing this book that this was my first exposure to the gift that I am. Spiritually, I serve as a living example of love, unconditional acceptance, and blessings. I am a vessel through which good energy flows.

Then, I forgot it all. I got away from all of it after graduating college. I let feelings control me. I let a need for validation control me. I needed proof that I was loved, instead of just trusting spirit to fill me up. I felt a feeling of missing out, and I felt numb. I filled this void with worldly love. I wanted the physical touch of a human. I wanted audible words of admiration and acknowledgement. I wanted the knowledge of geniuses, the utmost level of health, and the level of wealth of the richest. I wanted tangible happiness here, now, and at my disposal. My Subtle Quitter wasn't so subtle during this phase. I was completely disconnected from any higher being for a brief period of my life.

As my Subtle Quitter lost touch with religion *and* spirituality, I continued my chase: boys, job titles, achievements, things. You name it. For a while there, I did quit religion. I stopped asking and giving thanks for my blessings. Quantity took the place of quality, and I could never have enough. This created major blocks in my ability to feel and flow. I was missing connectedness, joy, simplicity, beauty, and the miracle of life. This complete disconnect brought me to my knees emotionally. I felt alone and lost. I spent energy on anger and sadness. I was wandering in confusion and seeking to quench a thirst that was simply insatiable.

I had lost my true self and purpose by chasing material feel-goods. I like to refer to this condition as 'Shiny Thing Syndrome.' Getting wrapped up in having and then eventually having it all taken away, knocked me back far enough to get a glimpse that I had lost touch with myself, my higher power, and my purpose in life. Furthermore, I saw that I was holding a grudge against God for never feeling present in my life. I understood that I was upset for never seeing cold hard evidence of His existence—as if Jesus was going to show up and show me the nail holes in his palms. I felt jealousy that others seemed to be buying in while I was missing out. Seeing this for myself floored me. I had to acknowledge and accept that I wasn't feeling Spirit because I was angry and resentful toward not feeling its presence. I learned how subtly my Subtle Quitter's disbelief existed. Something had to shift.

Ever-so-conveniently and unintentionally, during my recovery from divorce, I hired a life coach that flipped my spiritual self on her head! He is a spiritual warrior if I have ever met one. He would drop the God name left and right, but I knew he wasn't Catholic. It would bug me so one day I finally asked, "Why do you use 'God' when you refer to Spirit?" His matter-of-fact response shattered my perception that instant. "Because it's one syllable," he said. Mind blown. You can call your higher power 'The Chocolate Chip Pancake in the Sky' for all it matters, but what matters is that you have a relationship with a consciousness greater than you. I finally *got it!*

The Subtle Quitter became the Proud Creator! I was set free to find out how I could generate my own relationship to a force greater than me. On the most basic level, if you simply consider the consciousness of humanity, it is like a life force! Accepting that we are all truly one and intertwined at the heart can be palpable energy. Connecting to humanity as a whole takes me outside of myself and has me feeling close to a greater cause. I instantly recalled the feeling I had while leading at Kairos. I remember how deeply we all share the basic human needs of feeling loved, heard, known, and understood.

What I have created in my spiritual journey is connectedness. There is a sacred relationship I have to the hearts of others and the energy this earth and sky radiate. To brief you on anything I reference spiritually for the remainder of this book allow me to share my concept of the 'Boomerang Brigade.'

Regardless of your religious affiliation, we are all connected. Travel *anywhere* outside of your comfort zone long enough, and you will find your own flavor of truth in this: We are one. We are born of perfection. We are created to be full, whole, and complete beings, who are capable of love and understanding.

I may mention any of the following as interchangeable terms: The Universe, Spirit, God, Source Energy, or Whom(What)ever. Collectively and affectionately. I call this group the 'Boomerang Brigade.' I also love referring to them as 'The Powers-That-Be.'

The general idea of the Boomerang Brigade is

that *whatever* we put out there in the form of thoughts, beliefs, feelings, emotions, words, and actions is seen and heard by the Universe and comes back our way. What we put out comes back, period. We generate more of the energy we currently have. Consider that your Universe is like a giant, glass room comprised of mirrors, in which nothing is absorbed but instead, is reflected and flung *right back* at you! We attract people, places, things, and opportunities that serve us at the vibrational level that we are currently operating at. Raise your energy or vibrations: elevate your life.

Straight up, if we think we are blocking Spirit off, we are the only ones with a block. The Almighty is just hangin' tight until we get our wits about us and start trusting again. I came to see this for myself when I let go of worldly value and went back to finding joy in the interconnectedness of the human spirit and majesty of this planet. In my spiritual journey, the Subtle Quitter has become the Gracious Accepter. I have accepted that we are one. My interactions are much warmer now that I treat everyone I meet like I've known them forever. My life is much richer when everyone is a brother or sister in my eyes. I have gathered my wits about me. I feel connected to a greater presence.

No matter where you are on your own journey, the differences don't matter. We are all in it. We are all under the same umbrella. We are perfect as we are and one of the same. If you take one hundred percent responsibility for this, you are welcome to see divine greatness in anyone—even thine enemies.

Step outside of your 'the struggle is real' story, brush your teeth and put on your cape knowing that you are the vessel through which an amazing gift is to be delivered. You need to be in tip-top mental, emotional, physical, and spiritual shape in order to be dancing in the streets, delivering your greatness. Literally, shape up so you can ship out! Step out of struggle and into your flow. You have one. You may be tangled up in the weeds right now, but there is a path that you belong on. You have protection, you are loved, and help is just on the other side of asking for it.

Reflection Questions:

Have you ever taken the time to reflect on your spiritual journey?

Where are you?

Where do you want to be?

Do you believed you are loved?

Are you connected to a force greater than you?

Chapter 2

The Noble Quitter

I don't know who I disappointed more in my first real swing at quitting. When I decided to quit teaching, I was letting down a lot of folks, including myself. I knew I was going to be a teacher as far back as my elementary years. If you asked me as a ninth grader, I would have told you that I was going to be the middle/high school Physical Education and Health teacher at my alma mater. I stated it matter-of-factly because that is exactly how I related to it: just a matter of time.

I think that is where my white picket fence version of life began to take shape. I'd be a teacher. I'd get a husband. I'd have a handful of kids, and I would live a really safe, comfy, predictable life that I got to control. Honestly, I didn't even dream for more than that and didn't feel bad about it! To me it *was* living the dream, and I was going for it full steam ahead.

Being a teacher had been my only true vision

beyond basketball. I thought it was what I would do for the entirety of my life. In school, I would day-dream about being the teacher helping kids. I would be the coach I always wanted to have. I would be the one everyone could count on. I imagined my life as skipping through the halls with kids following my every instruction enthusiastically. I must admit, my dreams were glorious, so glorious in fact, that I did it. I became the PE and Health Teacher at good old WHS. I made my dream a reality.

It didn't take more than a few months for me to become disillusioned with public education. For starters, can you believe the kids didn't listen?! They weren't excited to be in school, and my passion didn't reach them at all. Try as I might, I couldn't break through to a large portion of them, and I hadn't developed the wherewithal to be okay with this. I hadn't yet had the breakthrough in my own life around trying to make everyone happy. Being unable to make a difference broke me in a way I hadn't anticipated, and I wasn't equipped to cope.

Bigger than my impact within school walls, Indiana had just passed a new system of merit based pay that kept teachers at entry-level salary. As a twenty-three-year-old, I found myself questioning how I would manage to live off of an entry-level salary for the rest of my life. The only way to get a pay raise was to go further into debt getting a higher degree, making myself unmarketable if I were to pursue a new school. To teach in another state meant new courses and certifications— more money. Looking into my projected future and seeing a capped salary capped my excitement for my chosen career path. I began to relate to the money game as a trap. I got choked up every time I talked about my financial future because I knew I had more than my income in student debt. It was an overwhelming, dead-end feeling, and I saw no solution in the educational system.

To sprinkle on more disenchantment, young teachers are comparable to high school freshman: the newbies. Before I knew it, I was a cross-country coach, basketball coach, and booster club sponsor spending nights and weekends at every extracurricular imaginable. I might have ended up with five more responsibilities if I hadn't learned to say no. While there truly was a part of me that loved it, there was another part of me that loved sleeping. There was even another part of me that desired a personal life, and it ripped my heart out because I felt so incredibly selfish about it. "I should want to help the kids," I thought. I felt like an entitled brat for still wanting my own freedom. There were so many days that a full-blown battle was occurring in my head and heart about how to be a committed, effective teacher while maintaining my passion, self, and sanity. I was in a crisis, going through every emotion every day, and if the job itself didn't exhaust me, feeling overextended did. The voice in my head would nag at me for wanting to run and hide, but it was all I could think of doing. I was so disempowered by this feeling, that quitting seemed to be the only option.

When I wrestled with leaving the dream job I had landed, I felt I was being self-centered. I struggled with having achieved exactly what I set out to do, and felt defeated that it wasn't the way I saw it in my dreams. So, there I was, a fresh, young gym teacher with seemingly everything I could ask for, and yet, I still found myself unfulfilled. I definitely thought there was something wrong with me and found myself questioning who I had become. I was lost as I pondered what I had committed the last ten years of my life to. I certainly felt the sting of guilt questioning if this was all there is, how I could not appreciate it, and if I was selfish for wanting more.

As I hung on, I developed resentment. I operated with a belief that teaching isn't about teaching and public education isn't about children. All I could see were all the things wrong with education. I now take responsibility for my perspective, but it was very much my reality as I lived it. As I tried to adapt, I quickly burnt out on it. I woke up and went to bed angry. I felt naïve for believing it was going to be all sunshine and rainbows. I thought I knew the work that teaching would be, and I was sorely mistaken. Worst of all, I felt jaded about my ability to make a difference. Over time, I noticed myself becoming more resigned and cynical.

Other than athlete, my identity resided in teacher and coach. I took so much pride in those titles. I really felt like *who I am* is a teacher. It was how I introduced myself and identified with the world. Who my soul was was a teacher, and I can honestly say that there are plenty of days I still feel that way. My brain and heart operate in a way that I had only ever known as 'teacher.' The biggest bridge to cross was taking a look at who I would actually be if I wasn't a teacher. Giving that up, voluntarily, no less, scared the ever-living crap out of me!

So, after many tears, I finally let go of the fear of disappointing others and risking being disliked for my decision. I owned my choice to leave my profession. It put knots in my stomach that I had spent four years and a fortune getting a degree that lasted me three years. I was truly disappointed in myself. I felt like I let down the ninth-grade version of myself who had put everything she had into making a positive impact as a teacher.

In the storm of resigning, I disappointed myself. I disappointed my mother. I disappointed faculty, administration, and students. I even felt like I disappointed the city that raised me. I had promised my life to be of service to this specific community, and I backed out on it. I felt as though I was leaving people in the dust by chasing bigger dreams. I felt like a sell-out. I felt like when the going got tough, I packed up and got going. Facing these feelings head on was absolutely gut-wrenching in the midst of it.

Needless to say, the choice was hard to make. Nonetheless, I call this version of my quitter the Noble Quitter. I made it pretty clear that I was disappointed by public education and that I refused to become an angry, resentful, sellout teacher who drags her feet all the way to retirement. I refused to shut off my mind and heart just to survive. I became aware that I had done that in basketball and the thought of doing it for the entirety of my life made me sick with anxiety and hopelessness. There is no punching in and out in teaching. It requires your entire heart and soul. I acknowledge every single teacher for their love of making a difference for children. Before losing my love completely, I told myself that I could, and would make the impact I wanted to make in some other way.

So, I became the Noble Quitter. I became the 'I don't need this shit' quitter. I made it look like the 'I won't put up with that negativity' quitter. To see this quitter in action looked like me refusing to succumb to 'the system.' I took a stand against public education and turned my nose up to traditional learning. I did my best to make it look noble, but I can tell you that I was relating to myself as a Runner. I was running away from something that I felt was bigger than me. I was running away because I felt so small, and there was nothing I could do to change what I felt was unjust. So, I quit. In teaching we call it resigning.

The day I resigned, I sat in my principal's office and cried. I cried because he trusted me, and I felt like a letdown. We were all tired. We were all in it together, but I was taking off. I didn't really need to explain myself to him or any other teacher. It was understood. In fact, once my resignation became public information, I got a lot of support and even a few high fives.

Taking this incredible leap of faith in myself is when I began to see the power of my own choices. Although I had very little knowledge about self-love at the time, I certainly felt it as a tidal wave of relief over me. I realized what I had done for myself. I had, for the very first time, made a very big choice for my well-being and my life, regardless of others' opinions. From the very last day of school, I left and never looked back. As hard as it was to do, it was just as rewarding to have done.

I have been asked to return to education a few times, and as graciously as possible given it a hard pass. Do I miss aspects of teaching and coaching? Of course! I had so much love for it. I have come to discover that I can make the same or a bigger impact in new, fresh ways. I have enjoyed the newfound freedom I have. The lesson I learned in being the Noble Quitter is that you really can choose outside of your perceived misery. I would like to share the idea that misery is frequently a perceived reality. There are plenty of teachers out there happily showing up to school knowing teaching is the fullest expression of themselves and their purpose. It is a noble career and for those who teach, I honor you. For me, becoming a teacher was a milestone in finding the fullest expression of myself, my passion, and my voice.

Sometimes, when we get really caught up in our circumstances, we lose sight of the bigger picture. The path narrows, and so does our vision. The perceived consequences of leaping into the unknown can be so threatening to our comfort that we avoid them. Instead of making a change, we convince ourselves that our predictable misery is better than an unpredictable, unknown future.

Therefore, we settle into believing that what is in front of us is all that is available. If I hadn't let go of teaching, I wouldn't have been able to grow into my completely realized dreams. I had to create space in my life for something new to show up.

Our hearts and minds operate similarly to vacuums. They don't stay empty for long. If we let go of something and create a void, by nature, something will fill it very quickly. We do this with jobs, relationships, habits, hobbies, etc. If you are in search of a fuller life, it is your responsibility to be more intentional about what fills those voids. When we fill them with comfort, we don't get much closer to our dream life. Keeping those voids open long enough for what is inside us to vacate, allows us to meet ourselves from a new perspective. Our authentic self begins to shine through and who we are becomes more apparent. Allowing the void to stay a void can be uncomfortable during the stages of self-discovery. Giving yourself the time to develop can be worth the reward of reaching your next level of freedom, power, or self-expression.

I am committed to being okay with the void, and I am committed to an unknown future. I found joy. I found freedom, and I came to realize that I am the only one who truly makes my choices. This was the first time I felt in control of my life and its direction. It was beyond scary to break past the barrier of my comfort zone. It required the armor of the Noble Quitter, but once I did it, I noticed that the rest of my life was still intact. All of the people I feared disappointing and losing as a result, were still in my life. I had my health and I actually had my sanity. I had made it all the way through a really scary life choice and in the process, I got my true first taste of self-love.

Reflection Questions:

What choices are you avoiding making because of the fear of disappointment?

Where does your concern for others' opinions keep you stuck?

What barriers of your comfort zone keep you where you are?

Chapter 3

The Tired Quitter

I came home on a typical week night, to find my husband having waited up for me. Surprised, I sat down on the couch and began to ask him about his day. He somberly turned off the TV and leaned forward in his chair. Hands folded, and eyes down, he told me he had something he needed to tell me. He had a different energy about him. It was in that moment that he told me he wanted a divorce. I remember him uttering the words "I'm tired of doing what everyone expects me to do." He was frustrated. He had had enough.

I could see, feel, and hear the difference in his being. He was finally taking charge and made a non-negotiable choice for himself and his happiness. It was the first time he had truly done that, at least in the six years I had known him. From where I sat, on the other end of the couch, it seemed as though he had agreed his life away. It was clear that he felt resentment. He said what he needed to say and made it clear that marriage was a mistake. Whatever it took to wake him up, something surely did.

We were college sweethearts. I played basketball, and he played baseball. He was tall, handsome, slightly goofy, and easy going—just the way I like 'em. College life was simple. I went to his games with my girls, and we rooted for our men. There was a gang of us dating a gang of them, and it was all cheers and beers. After graduation, we both moved home but made it work for the time being. I fell in love with his family, and they fell in love with me. I was invited to holidays and family vacations, and I was living a dream. Eventually, I successfully linked our fun-loving families, and I was in all my glory. It was everything I could have imagined growing up, being the daydreamer I was. As our relationship deepened, he supported me through my struggles with teaching and my decision to leave. Life felt easy with John, and building my picture-perfect life around him seemed just as simple. Each stage of the relationship flowed into the other because I became more and more willing to go with his flow.

When he told me he didn't want to live in my town, I moved to his. It didn't even occur to me that he may not have been trying to move in together. I knew he loved his neighborhood, and so did I, so it wasn't a major concern for me to compromise that choice. As he took four plus years to ask me to marry him, he would tell me he wanted to be sure, so I waited. Along the way I would question his timeline, but he would simply remind me that he wanted to be ready on his own time. I was positive that he was sure when he took me ring shopping one random afternoon. With my mother-in-law by my side, I picked my own ring. The two of us were like giddy school girls about my finally joining the family. In my mind, I had arrived at the rest of my glorious life.

Together six years and married six months, we were cruising along in life. We were house shopping. We were planning family vacations. We had discussed starting a family soon. We were planning life. The plans took a hard left when I came home that Wednesday night and I had new facts to face. What was created over six years had ended in a forty-five-minute conversation. Our marriage was over. The picket fence vision I had created for my life was suddenly bulldozed. Everything I spent twenty-six years picturing had vanished.

Our relationship ended that night, but I cannot say I was at all prepared to be twenty-seven, divorced, and now...single. I lost a husband and a huge family that I loved so dearly. I was asked quite often in those following months what I would do. Where would I go? What now? What's next? All the while, when I considered my future, I saw nothing. Blackness. Darkness. Nothingness.

Being the woman that I am, I was determined to be strong about this. I was determined to be okay and not let this divorce define me. I would be strong. I would be fine. I would overcome. So I forged on. I worked long hours, went home to pack up my old life every night, transferred jobs, moved apartments, and worked more. I tried with all my might to just keep chugging along.

I was confused. I was scared. I felt rejected, and I didn't know what I could have possibly done differently, or better. I felt rejected for being me. I felt like my intense passion, love, and loyalty made this go wrong, as if I drove him away. After the divorce, it took months of working toward understanding myself for me to realize I wasn't really being myself in marriage. I was compromising who I was, where I wanted to live, and how I wanted to live in order to have that picture-perfect picket fence. I was trying to live up to all I thought I should be, as opposed to anything I wanted to actually be. For the first time I understood what my husband meant. I was tired of doing what I thought I was supposed to be doing.

John's words have resonated in my head at least a few times: "I'm tired of doing what everyone expects me to do." I've done a lot of reflecting since divorce, and I can confidently confirm that I was spending most of my days living up to other people's expectations of me. I was so outcome driven that I never stopped to decide if we were compatible as life partners. I was working to be perfect. I was working to have 'made it.' I was working to keep up an image of perfection I had created and I had had enough. I, too, got tired of doing what others thought I should be doing. The funniest part of all of it? No one actually told me I had to approach life in this specific order or time frame. Some had even tried to slow me down! Shocker, right?! No one was putting that pressure on me, besides me. I had convinced myself that this way was right and any other way was wrong. I was more committed to the *image* of who I was than who I *actually* was. I saw that I was in a relationship with myself. I was working to create the illusion of achievement, success, and happiness, instead of just living and being it.

When John left me, I had to completely re-evaluate what I was living for. I was forced to decide what was most important to me, and I could see how much I had morphed away from who I was, in an effort to convince him of marriage. I thought I was being me, but I was busy trying to be marriage material. My inner feminist cringes at the idea now, but I didn't see this for what it was while I was in the midst of it. I was simply committed to being the best girlfriend, fiancé, and wife I ever knew how to be. Only from the perspective of reflection did I understand how far away from my core I had drifted.

The last time I saw John was the night we broke up. I packed up, moved on, and spent the next year learning me again. I hadn't known Single Abby in over a decade. I didn't know Independent Abby. I didn't know Abby who knew her worth and I had *no idea* who Abby as woman was.

This journey and evolution has been exhilarating and enlightening. I am still learning me every single day.

I began choosing things that are extensions and expressions of me and my true essence. I can say that the year after divorce was the wackiest roller-coaster I have ever been on. The highs were the highest, and the lows were the scariest. I shed layers and layers of expectations, and whatever I was still holding on to, I worked on letting go.

By asking for a divorce, my husband set me free. My husband let me be. I got a second chance and a swift kick in the dupa to get to livin'! As I spent the next few days cooped up, crying and/or sleeping in 'our' apartment, my guardian angel whispered over my shoulder, "Wake up sleepy-head, you have a life to live."

During divorce, I became the Tired Quitter who was sick of the charade. The Tired Quitter was frustrated, exhausted, and defeated. She had a soft punch and lackadaisical energy. She simply surrendered her efforts in being someone she wasn't. Over the next few months, I didn't know how to be. I was lost trying to navigate my newfound singledom. As I have grown out of the grief, I quit putting unnecessary pressure on myself to look, or be perfect. I quit trying to have my life look like a magazine cut out. I stopped chasing happiness and started cultivating it in the very moment.

What I learned while being the Tired Quitter is that I am perfect however I am. I am full. I am whole. I realized that I actually know a thing or two about myself and what I want in life. I am complete as I am and have no need to become someone else.

I came to understand that even in hurt, everything in life is a blessing. Whether it is there to teach me a lesson or enrich my life with laughter, every single person, place, and event is a blessing. I quit dressing it up, and now I just live blessed. I live happy. I live in love.

I've never been able to turn off my dreams, but I had gotten too afraid to chase the big ones…because what on earth would I do if I actually caught them? I noticed myself becoming a figurative and literal pack rat. I was holding onto medals, trophies, and pictures, galore. I would always recall memories of achievement to quiet the chatter of my inner critic. It was my only access to feeling accomplished, and I was dead scared of leaving all that I had obtained behind in order to go for all that I had dreamed of. It is metaphorically comparable to trying to stay in high school because you love it, while also trying to go to college. You simply can't. They cannot coexist. You finish one and it is time to move on to the other. Objectively, it seems simple and matter-of-fact. Subjectively, we attach meaning, emotion, and worth to it. Phases in life have expiration dates. When we try to hold on to everything, we are the ones caught in the middle. Going for my biggest dreams meant leaving some of my fulfilled ones behind. That white picket fence was an expired dream and from it, I was chasing happy every day. Today, I live it.

Reflection Questions:

What are you holding onto that may actually be holding you back?

How is your 'white picket fence' fantasy dictating your dreams, goals, and version of yourself?

What pressures of perfection are causing you to negotiate yourself, life, and ultimate vision of personal success?

Do your biggest dreams scare you?

Chapter 4

The Jaded Quitter

I cannot say there was a single event in which the Jaded Quitter was developed, but I can say there was an extremely specific event in which she was discovered.

At a very young age, I believe it was elementary school, my dad showed me *The Secret*—a documentary about the law of attraction. It described how we can intentionally draw on our desires to create the life we want. It opened my little brain up to the power of my thoughts! I understood that I could create whatever I wanted in life as long as I spoke the truth and went for it. I trust that this is how I became a college athlete and teacher. I have achieved a lot in life trusting my abilities, in order to turn my dreams into a reality.

I also believe seeing *The Secret* is when my "save the world mission" started. I call it the "save the world mission" because I believe that having a positive impact will create the ripple effect so rapidly that it will occur in tidal waves! I genuinely believe that anyone can do any-thing they want. It has become a personal endeavor of mine to instill in others that they are the masters of their own lives. The most basic, emotional human needs are to feel loved, heard, known, and understood. As a life coach, I have been hell-bent on training others to have their needs met in such a way that they are empowered to go for the fullest version of their lives, only more rapidly producing the ripple effect of positive impact. No matter how each particular endeavor ended up, I have noticed my own pattern in my life; any meaningful work or relationship that I have taken on has had some potential for my "save the world mission."

To back up a bit, what my young brain did with this newly learned information was formulate ideas about how to make a positive impact. I believed I could be friends with everyone and usually, I was, or tried to be. I have, of course, screwed this up in my human nature, but I have made a solid attempt. Over the years, I joined as many clubs and sports as possible. I did as much as possible. I enjoyed life as much as possible. I didn't buy into stereotypes that there was any one way to be, like a jock, or a nerd, or an artist. I certainly didn't believe that we don't all relate to each other. I could sketch as well as I could shoot a basketball. I could play the saxophone as well as I could ace a math test. I did not believe in limitations; therefore, I did everything I could.

As I grew, my ninth-grade brain decided that the most positive impact I could make was through teach-ing. I set my sights and it was game over. As stated previously, it was just a matter of time before I achieved my goal.

In the meantime, I went through high school at the top of my game, and played basketball in college. I believe this was my first experience in formulating the Jaded Quitter. College basketball was tough. I thought I was tough, and it brought me down. The world outside of little old Whiting didn't seem to care who I was, and no one owed me any favors. I got a big dose of humble pie when I tore my ACL two days before my sophomore season started. It was the closest I have ever come to experiencing depression. I lost all my worth in a single layup. I had never been hurt. I had never broken a bone and all of a sudden, I couldn't play the sport that I had dedicated my life to.

I was now laid up, watching practice from the sidelines, and prepping for invasive surgery that would take months to recover from. Consider this an identity crisis. I had only ever known myself as a student-athlete. Athlete was my favorite identity. I was proud before, and now, I was nothing. All I had left was my work ethic, and it could not heal me. In fact, it hurt me. I worked so hard to recover that I tore my knee more, resulting in five knee surgeries over the course of six years.

The Jaded Quitter made me realize that I am no longer invincible. I am stoppable, and I had the 'holy shit, I'm actually human' moment. I am susceptible to failure, and I was not okay with it. I was not used to it. It had become second nature to me to succeed. I worked hard for the following three years. The harder

I worked, the more forcefully I tried to control outcomes. This pattern only further created the identity of the Jaded Quitter.

At that age, I did not know how to quit basketball, so I didn't. Like I had known to do previously, I struggled through to its dreary end. Like any team situation, my suffering was a cancer that I was not taking responsibility for. I was causing suffering everywhere and for everyone. I did not see it this way because I was relating to myself as a victim. I was a victim of my injury from the moment it happened to the last minute of the last game. The last day of my senior basketball season may have been more monumental than my graduation day from college! I was free from my self-inflicted misery, but I left with some literal and figurative scar tissue. The Jaded Quitter started collecting evidence for a developing belief that life is not fair, and I am not enough as myself.

As I stated earlier, I landed a teaching job and got my first glimpse that the education system wasn't for me. I began to put together blueprints and a business plan for opening my own gym. My logic was that if I couldn't stand teaching gym in schools, I could make it available elsewhere in the world. I worked out the details for a year with local city staff and believed it was going to become a reality. It was only through the newspaper that I found out the building I had been planning this project around was given to a corporation instead. My Jaded Quitter concluded this as more proof, another failure for the books. "Give it up, Ab," my inner quitter whispered. She nagged at my raw heart. I really began to give up on my dreams of making a difference.

I decided to stick with my second-best passion of working in a gym by joining a corporate gym chain. At this point, my edges had softened. My poignant persistence to make a positive impact had been reduced to settling into a gym management position. I had struck out enough to just want a break from the game. I had gone after an easy, non-threatening job that I could clock in and out of.

In due time, I would come to see what corporate life was all about, and discovered that it wasn't my long-term goal. At that point, I had been dating my college sweetheart for six years and we were getting married. You already know how that one ends. I had literally let go of every goal other than becoming a kick-ass wife and mom. I had let life's challenges wear me down. A young woman, who once aspired to save the world, had accepted that maybe she could simply make her own world comfortable enough to live in.

I had given up on creating an extraordinary life for myself until a member of my gym approached me about a network marketing company that I had never heard of. It was a vegan health and wellness company and all it took was a seven-day sample of their anti-aging face line for me to sign up and jump in head first. I was beyond eager to have a new flame ignited in my soul. My undying competitor craved a new challenge, and this opportunity couldn't have come at a better time. Newly engaged, I saw this as a chance to pay for the wedding. As I climbed the company ladder lighting fast, my vision grew. I saw the promise of building this business into a lifestyle of being a stay-at-home mom with a thriving side hustle. This opportunity married my passion for helping others with my desire of being my own boss. It was perfect for me and I was proud to be a part of it. The Jaded Quitter got sidelined at this time, because I was a woman with a clear vision about where her life was going: up and fast.

I became so enlivened by my new passion and possibility that I joined a twelve-month ontological life coach training program in order to improve my leadership skills. I was so committed to making it to the tippy top of my skincare company that I was willing and ready to break through any barriers I had, in order to lead hundreds of others to their dreams. I figured that in order to run a multimillion dollar business, it was necessary to be in tip-top shape as a network marketing sponsor, coach, and leader. I was more than ready to get started in my life coach training program. Three days before my program started, John asked me for our divorce.

Sirens, bells, and whistles were ringing in my head. My Jaded Quitter had a field day! More evidence! More proof! *All* the more reason to give up on any dream I could ever conjure up from here on out. My last standing dream of motherhood just got pushed back indefinitely. The purpose of my network marketing business crumbled. My general drive for success halted. Cue total devastation. Cue the complete loss of worth and purpose.

As I dealt with the grief of divorce, everything in

my life had a chokehold on me. I began to resent my nine-to-five. I tried dating before I was ready. I was busying myself in ridiculous ways to quiet my thoughts and numb my pain. None of it was working, and it certainly wasn't helping. In my grieving, I reflected about who I became in marriage. I came to understand that I hadn't been myself. Even in the aftermath, I wasn't truly being myself for a while. As a toxic combination of the Tired and Jaded Quitter, I didn't have enough memory or wherewithal to draw on who I remembered myself to be. I lost my spark, faith, and determination. In my recovery, I got a chance to see how slowly I morphed away from who I was. Detail by minute detail, I had let go of who I was and what was most important to me, and I had no idea how to get it all back.

The Jaded Quitter collected enough evidence to convince me that my "save the world mission" was in fact hopeless. I sure did believe her. I stared at my list of failures, and my resentment toward my passion grew. I began to self-criticize with questions like, 'Why help others if it can all go away in an instant? Why get excited if it can all go away in an instant?' Why plan? Why care? Why Try?' So, the Jaded Quitter stopped caring, stopped planning, and stopped trying. It was a dark time. I had truly quit.

Finally meeting my Jaded Quitter triggered a good, long cry. One of those 'ugly cries' in which you really let it all out.

It was in a three-day life coaching forum in which I stood face to face with the trunk full of disappointing evidence that I had collected proving that I cannot, in fact, achieve my "save the world mission." I had to unpack it, look at each item I had saved, and toss it out. I found myself sad and repulsed that I had let life's challenges beat me down hard enough to surrender what I am most committed to from the deepest depths of my soul.

I recalled that elementary school girl who loved everyone and truly believed in anyone's ability to achieve anything. I had forgotten the power of creating one's own desires. In coaching, I distinguish the concept of being 'a stand' for my clients. I explain that I am, much like a flagpole, a strong and unwavering stand for what they tell me they want. No matter what storms we face together, my clients can count on me to stand strong, with and for them. In my clients' transformations, I have them explore what they are a stand for in their own lives. Together we generate their freedom and power to build a strong foundation to stand on their own. I remembered that who I am is a stand for positive impact. I am a stand for love in this world. I am a stand for people being full, whole, and complete, and *actually* believing it. I am a stand for people accepting who they are, accepting the gift that they are, and unleashing their enormous hearts to this world!

The moment I met the Jaded Quitter, I quit her. I saw her resignation about life. Her resentment for the world was toxic. I saw how she had stopped believing in and trusting others. She wore her 'life's not fair' attitude on her sleeve and had little faith in the idea that life works out for the best. Instead of believing and doing, she quit making any attempts at her 'save the world' mission. She held this massive grudge against possibility for constantly slipping through her tightly gripped fingers. As soon as I met this quitter, I saw how powerfully she was holding my back from everything I wanted in life. Enough was enough of her running the show. I had wasted sufficient time feeling sorry for myself, and it was time to get back on my white horse. I have been riding her ever since.

Reflection Questions:

Have you met your version of the Jaded Quitter?

How many 'hits' has this identity taken?

What evidence have you collected in your trunk of disappointments?

What is your version of the 'life's not fair' context?

Have you caught yourself giving up on others, or giving up on the 'Boomerang Brigade?'

Where in your life have you lost trust?

What "save the world mission" have you surrendered?

Are you willing to let go of your perceived losses in order to get back on your mission?

Chapter 5

The Self-Righteous Quitter

This quitter can be seen in different phases of my life, such as teaching and gym management, but she has her own flavor of 'I don't need this shit!' This quitter only surfaced as a result of the others, and is quite the badass. I noticed the victim role that I was playing, and the Self-Righteous Quitter rose from the ashes of hurt Abby. She showed up with her sword and cape, and I stood behind her as she fought my battles for me.

The real transition I made when I fully stepped into Self-Righteous Quitter was taking my time back. After divorce, I did a lot of figurative looking in the mirror. With the guidance and support in my life coach training program, I took a lot of responsibility for the way my life had gone. I stopped being mad at everyone else, but I was still pretty upset with myself. I was upset that I had been the key player in the way my life had gone, and that I had been so blind to the way I was creating it.

Looking in the mirror exposed the power leaks all over my life, and Ms.Self-Righteous Quitter had had enough!

My Self-Righteous Quitter decided to take all of my time back! I swung from one side of the pendulum to the other. In a matter of five months I had quit my successful and growing network marketing company. At my corporate management job, I demoted myself from upper management, later to demote myself from management completely, all the way back down to part-time front desk reception. I became stingy with my time because I knew it was time to start deciding how I wanted to spend the rest of my life. I finally understood that the pen is in my hand and I am writing the story. With this new perspective, I certainly became self-righteous. I had a fond relationship with the Self-Righteous Quitter. She became a hero of mine. I was on a quitting spree and my middle fingers way up to anyone who didn't respect my choices. Nobody was going to tell me what to do! In this phase, I quit people pleasing. I quit caring about others' expectations of me. I quit saying "Yes!" to every request. I quit compromising my standards and priorities. I openly told people to put their opinions where the sun doesn't shine, and I threw a match on my past, literally. I burned any memory I had of marriage and shredded any leftovers I found over time.

I became hyper-focused on my well-being and my mental health. I had become hyper-focused and hyper-aware. Well, honestly, just hyper. It didn't feel exactly right, but I told myself that it was normal while going through such a huge life transformation. Every move generated momentum, so I never pumped the breaks. I let the Self-Righteous Transformation Train roll on.

I let the Self-Righteous Quitter run her course. I took my time back. I took my life back. I took my power back. As a result, that pendulum swing leveled out. In due time, I was able to make some more sound decisions that moved me forward on my path to my fullest life.

As I quit everything, I made room for my own priorities. I fully owned my entrepreneurship as a life coach and began getting clients. I ended my rebound relationship and swore myself single. I booked my first solo travel vacation to Hawaii and experienced myself as capable again. I booked a trip to California to learn how to snowboard and decided to move there instead. I rid myself of about fifty percent of my material possessions and felt a hundred pounds lighter. A month after deciding, I had made it happen. I moved to California and began creating the hell out of my life! I needed the Self-Righteous Quitter. I needed her in order to become me again. She supported me through a lot of letting go. I never truly understood how much of my past I was holding onto, but letting go of it has allowed me to go for everything that is possible in life.

In my transformation, I have shifted from the Self-Righteous Quitter to the Powerful Woman. I see my role as Creator in my life so clearly that I have taken one hundred percent responsibility for the quality and direction of it. The phase of Self-Righteous Quitter was necessary. I needed to learn how to set standards, expectations, boundaries and consequences. In doing so, I have become so free to be me that the only permission I require is my own. Letting go and choosing powerfully are tools to live an extraordinary life as a whole, complete person. With the power I got back as the Self-Righteous Quitter, I began to create my life as a reflection of what is in my heart and I allowed it to flourish. To this day, I create the life I love.

Reflection Questions:

What do you think a little time in the mirror would reveal to you?

What is holding you back, crowding your space, and cramping your style?

What would a Self-Righteous Quitter make room for in your life?

What do you need support in letting go of?

If you had more wiggle room in your life to show up as yourself, who would you be?

Chapter 6

The Enlightened Quitter

Very much like the Jaded Quitter, all it took was seeing my unlovable story for the enormous cancer that it was for me to decide to end the cycle. 'Stories' are the conversations we have with ourselves that we often don't know we are having. These stories dictate our life and our perception of the world. They are also known as contexts, lenses, goggles, perspectives, or viewpoints. They are a natural part of the human condition. We all have them, but we add our own flavor to them. They are unique to us, and, yet, we can all relate.

An intention of this book is to help you clarify the stories that you have created about yourself and operate from. I invite you to consider that these stories are simply your perception, and not necessarily accurate. For example, when I shared with my mom and sister how unlovable I considered myself to be, they laughed at me. "You are SO lovable, Abigail!" Emily gently offered between her giggles, but I did not agree. I was even a little upset when they laughed at a personal issue that has been a real struggle for me throughout my life. I was so convinced about my unlovability that I was actually mad that they DIDN'T agree with me! Talk about wanting to be right! I got over being upset when I took a look from a fresh perspective.

It was another three-day ontological forum that created the perfect storm in which my unlovable story was exposed. I already had fourteen months of ontological coach training. You would have thought this story would have occurred to me by now— but it hadn't. It didn't occur to me that it was just that, a story, because I was so convinced that it was fact. It was a non-negotiable fact that I had created about myself at the ripe old age of four. At that age, I made the decision that something was wrong with me, and it became part of who I thought I was.

Sitting in a room for three days straight with a hundred and ten others from various backgrounds, cultures, careers, income brackets, and families, sharing their stories, I got it. I got why my mom and sister laughed. I watched these other amazing humans doubt their greatness and limit their possibility *with their thoughts!* In that forum, I gained access to humanity. I really *got* that we are all operating in the face of some flavor of fear, and I noticed for myself, it is the fear of rejection.

No one is fear-proof. Some of us are courageous enough to face our fears, but they exist nonetheless. I learned that these one hundred and ten other people were just as afraid of judgement and rejection as I was. The difference about the energy in this room was that we weren't making any effort to try to hide it. We were open. We were raw. I was them, and they were me. I gained access to my own heart through the hearts of others. In this storm of authenticity, I stood back and watched it swirl. I watched the emotions flow like water through its cycle. Condense, rain down, puddle, evaporate. I saw the fleeting nature of it. I saw our part in the storm. I saw my part in my own storm.

My unlovable story ran my life from youth. I saw the role I played. I saw the role my inner child played. I saw how I let my inner child dictate how the adult version of me perceived the world, made choices, and reacted to circumstances. Whew-ee!!! Recognizing that I was letting my past and fears run the show was enough for me. I momentarily mourned the years I had wasted, wiped my tears, and truly understood and accepted in that moment that I am not who I thought I was—and thank God. I get to just be. I am whole. I am complete. I am perfect. I am actually nothing, and from nothing, anything can be created.

During this storm, I became the Enlightened Quitter. I truly got that our word is our truth and our truth is our reality. We can change our word, therefore, we can change our reality - and so I did. In that moment, I chose that I was incredible. I was extraordinary. I was and am, love and loved. That is what I have become and what my life has become.

As you can imagine, from all this self-realization,

this Enlightened Quitter felt, well, enlightened! I finally got how much of my time, energy, and life I was spending fixing myself and trying to become 'good enough.' From the unlovable perspective, there simply is no 'good enough.' I understood that no matter what I would ever do or try to do or achieve in life, it would never be the thing that tipped the scale of my happiness. The feeling of 'having done it' didn't last for long, and it kept me in a pattern of working to create a feeling. All my efforts were attempts to feel loved, accepted, and worthy. For as long as I related to myself as less than, that is what I would always be. Even in racking up worldly successes, I would never be enough until I personally made the choice that I *am* enough, so that is exactly what I did. I chose that my worth was no longer contingent on a title, achievement, relationship, or creation. Everything I would do, I would do my best to create from the essence of who I am, and as an expression of what is in my heart.

The session ended that Sunday. On Monday, I called my life coach, my inner child specialist, and my support group sponsor. I acknowledged their amazing roles in my life. I thanked them for getting me to where I was, but let them know that I wouldn't be needing them anymore. I explained that I had taken all this on to fix what I thought was wrong with me and that I had discovered there is nothing wrong! Some departures went better than others, but I completed them, nonetheless.

I spent that entire Monday relaxing and smiling. I had let go of my fixing mission, so I had nowhere to be and nothing to do. For the first time ever, I experienced what it truly meant to be present. I may even dare to say the life of my dreams began to take shape in the following days. That week, I started this book. That month, I reached the most clients I've had, and had my highest paid coaching month to date. A few months later, I began dating again. I began to choose life powerfully as opposed to filling voids with comfort or fear. Overall, my life began to blossom from a brand-new place. I began to *actually believe* I could have it all again *and* that I was deserving of it. I started appropriate actions to attain it all! A new life, a full life, a life without mysterious power leaks, and all because I let go of the slew of grudges and stories from the past.

There was a 'building up to' in those three days, but I broke down every imaginary barrier I had built up over the course of my life. I allowed myself to be wrong about my harsh opinion of myself. I saw and ended a twenty-eight-year story that I was unlovable. I rocked my foundation, and my little house of cards came crashing down. From this new place, I have been able to build a sturdy home with a stronger base, and no ceilings.

The Enlightened Quitter was fun. She allowed me access to acceptance and peace of mind. My Enlightened Quitter served me greatly in seeing, loving, and unleashing my greatness. She was courageous as hell, but, we can't forget, still a quitter.

All while I was practicing quitting, I produced some phenomenal conceptual breakthroughs in the way I thought about life. I finally saw that major story about how unlovable and unworthy I was for what it was. So, as I practiced all this new quitting, I begin to see the gaps in my self-worth and began to fill them with self-love.

Reflection Questions:

What stories do you tell yourself, about yourself?

What is the first memory you have as a child of thinking something was wrong with you?

What is the story you made up about yourself from there?

How has this story stopped you in life?

How does it stop you today?

How long do you intend to let that story run your life?

How much longer are you going to pretend it doesn't?

Without your story, who do you say that you are?

Part Three

Conceptual Quitting

Chapter 1

People Pleasing

After every breakthrough I have had in my transformation, I am stopped dead in my tracks when I realize the profound impact any single character trait can have on so many aspects of life. The effects of each one were so subtle that, without taking a look in the mirror to distinguish them, it just felt like my life was slowly unraveling. I felt like a complete victim of the 'life's not fair' context that I existed in. To distinguish all these different traits from each other took away their power. To call them out for what they were, to declare "they are not me," generated freedom. I got to create Abigail as a woman, and that became access to self-expression. Meeting my various quitters was essential to my evolution. By quitting these character traits, I was called forth into learning, owning, loving, accepting, and sharing myself as who I want to be.

Who I want to be is me.

When you explore the third part of this book, I invite you to figuratively sit in front of the mirror. We all have survival mechanisms in place to withstand the events life throws at us. In this section of conceptual reflection, get to know you. Get to know the survival skills you have set in place to protect your heart.

So far, I have covered some pretty specific examples of quitting. Quitting people pleasing was a very conceptual and pivotal moment of my life. It was one of my first breakthroughs and one of the most meaningful. Breaking through the need to please others reignited my passion for power and freedom. Before seriously letting go of others' expectations, there was no room for my own. This created a constant sense of overwhelming and personal disappointment.

Evidence of my people pleasing is littered throughout this book. The whole structure was set up on a foundation of needing to be accepted, wanting to be loved unconditionally, and being super fearful of abandonment. I feared that giving up people pleasing meant giving up being accepted by others. I feared that becoming powerful and free would actually create loneliness and isolation. I realize now that this compromising relationship with power and freedom kept me from choosing a life that is an expression of what I am truly passionate about. Once I quit concerning myself with others' expectations, I really discovered the expectations

I have for myself. My favorite example of this was my very first swing at 'saying no.'

My family is known for its charitable community work. I was raised volunteering and often loved it. It was always a family affair and I love, I mean LOVE my family. Every summer we would volunteer at the local symphony. We ran the concession stand and sold 50/50 raffle tickets to help raise money for charities. I didn't even make plans for summer Saturday nights. I knew I was working the symphony, and attendees knew it would be the Gazda gals walking around, both arms swaying above our heads shouting, "50/50 tickets!!!! Get cha 50/50 tickets!"

The summer after divorce, I would've rather crawled under a rock than gone marching out in front of hundreds. I had no interest in walking up to those who raised me up from diapers to get the hand-on-shoulder with head-tilted, "Hey, how ya doin', hun?" The thought of reminding people that I was doing alright with every ticket I sold made my teeth grind. While I was sure their intentions were good, I just wasn't up for it. A family event that used to bring me joy now became a chore, and the Abby that was showing up was not one who would attract ticket sales.

This brings me to my breakthrough. Well, this brings me to the breakdown. I had to tell my family, 'No.' I had to stand face to face with my crippling fear of disappointing the people I love the most and risk disapproval. With my stomach in my throat, I went one by one telling my mom, aunt, and grandma that I didn't want to work the symphony anymore. I didn't explain. I didn't justify. I didn't wish-wash about it. I just did. I drew the line and stepped over it. This simple step felt like jumping off a dang cliff in the moment, but, I did it. I said no, and, get this, they *accepted* it! They accepted it simply and further shared their love with me! In my heart, the fourteen-year old band nerd with throbbing gums leapt for joy!

I felt heard and understood. They got where I was and respected the boundary I had set up! After an insane amount of relief rushed over me, so did a wave of self-love. I got exactly what I was going for! I felt powerful and free! For the first time I could recall, I had simply set up a personal boundary that didn't require an explanation or excuse. As I write this example now, I laugh about how serious I was about not wanting to work a family event, but it clearly meant more to me than that. This example was a way of being for me. It represented the teacher that always said yes and the girlfriend who bent and molded to what her boyfriend wanted. The pattern of responding "yes" to everything was an undercurrent in my life that was discreetly drifting me further and further away from the shore of my dreams.

Confronting the fear of standing up for myself freed me up to look at where else I had this way of being set up in my life. I took a closer look at what I was up to in the world. I began to see that ninety percent of what I was doing was to people please—to be liked, accepted, trusted, and admired. I could see very clearly that I was serving others to gain approval as opposed to actually fulfilling a purpose for personal pleasure. Furthermore, I was working to be loved by people who already love me. It took letting go of pleasing, and then setting up boundaries, to see the insane amount of imaginary pressure that I was putting on myself!

During my breakthrough in people pleasing, I was introduced to the idea of the bigger 'what for.' When learning to become a life coach we were told that 'why' is a dirty word in coaching. As we practiced with each other, I saw right then that if asked *why* I was doing something, I would defend my actions like a lioness defends her cub. If I was asked *what for*, I took an introspective look at the places I was choosing from. With all this new clarity, a clear line was drawn between choosing from fear or desire. Cue the groundbreaking moment. I became connected to the purpose of my actions. I learned that I am the one with the choice.

Spoiler alert: these characteristics do not go away. I spent twenty-eight years people pleasing! Just because I don't work the symphony anymore doesn't make me people-pleaser-proof. Instead, I now take responsibility for my need to please. There's a little secret about transformation that many don't see right away: we are who we are and we are not who we are not. The automatic ways our brains developed growing up shapes the conclusions that we make about life. The series of events and relationships in our childhoods further create us to be exactly how we are today. Every minute of our lives got us here, and we wouldn't be the same without them. Therefore, decades of reinforcement don't dissipate simply because we know about our behaviors and attitudes. The experience is much like breaking the habit of nail biting. The action has become automatic, but awareness of it alone gives us the power to make intentional choices and commitments outside of what we have been conditioned to believe or do. Meeting all of my quitters has empowered me to choose a life outside of running and hiding. My quitters did not just go away because I identified them! Truthfully, I danced with them for a while before I gained more confidence in being myself. I developed my identity separate from my fears and insecurities. In fact, if I had listened to my quitters any longer, you would not be reading this book!

In light of my breakthrough, I stay one step ahead of my quitters. I choose not to agree and suffer through an experience purely out of obligation. I choose not to just go through the motions anymore because I now know that those involved are not getting my best work. Well, they may be getting great work but *really* crappy energy, which is extremely counterproductive to the cause. I keep a very intentional look out for that feeling now. I keep a look out for that self-inflicted pressure I feel when I am making choices about which projects I want to invest my time, energy, and commitment.

Who you are and where you're coming from in your efforts matters much more than what it is you are doing or how it gets done. *Who* you are in your commitments determines *how* it gets done. This never goes away. Taking responsibility for this equation gives you your power back. Being 'Abigail' instead of 'people pleaser' gave me back the power of choice, and this option is available to anyone willing to take a look for themselves. This awareness allows you to align your commitments and actions with your intentions. If practiced and played with, it frees you up to live and serve from a place of being full, whole, and complete, instead of having resentment, obligation, and guilt. This creates an opportunity to choose meaningful work and play! I can work the symphony again because I now choose to with energy, excitement, and vitality. Who I have created myself to be determines how I show up to life. I no longer choose people pleaser. I choose Abigail.

Reflection Questions:

Where in your life do you see a pattern of people pleasing?

Do you find yourself sacrificing your needs, for the sake of pleasing others?

If you drew your own line between your fears and desires, on which side do each of your obligations fall?

If you were operating with full freedom and power, what would you chose to be doing as a true expression of yourself and your passions?

What is most important to you in life?

Chapter 2

Trying to Have 'Made it'

For those of you who have spent time exploring self-discovery, I'm sure you became quickly aware that life is a journey. There's no one 'made it' moment. Well, except for the final one, and if you have read this far into the book, I trust that you aren't rushing to that one!

Anyone reading have a dream board? I do. I've had a few. When I started my network marketing business, my dream board had a Mercedes, the title of the level that I wanted to hit with my company, a man at the top of a mountain and an insanely large lake house. You know those dream boards. In business, we call these driving factors our 'Whys.'

These images were meant to motivate us in our times of fear and doubt. They served as reminders not to quit when it got uncomfortable. They were meant to display 'Why' we were doing what we were doing and to what end. My most recent dream board had an open field of flowers, the word joy, a landscape of mountains, and the phrase 'Born on Purpose.'

There is no right or wrong about one's desires.

Somewhere in the middle of creating those two dream boards, I distinguished a difference in how I was wanting and how I was measuring success. Originally, I was chasing physical things that would represent to others and myself that I had 'made it.' I have come to call those the "Shiny Things." Hence, I introduce to you the "Shiny Thing Syndrome." I found myself fixated on my future success and an image of perfection. That man atop the mountain represented reaching ultimate success and happiness.

My favorite analogy of this is parenthood. Relating to it as a mountain top experience would be like having that child and saying "Sweet! Parenthood! I got there! Whew, I can relax now!" I think we can all say that birth is not parenthood. It is the very beginning of a journey that leads to a lifelong commitment to the experience of parenthood and *all* that it entails. It is an ongoing experience that shape shifts with age. The same analogy could go for a wedding day, in relation to a marriage.

Of course, every story is unique, but there is a difference in surviving the climb and thriving on the journey. In retrospect, it seemed to be a common theme throughout my life. I noticed it was a natural human condition to be chasing this imaginary point in life without intention. There is always a 'chasing the end' mindset operating. I was rushing to get to a point in life where I could relax, or call it enough, and feel as though I could retire my efforts of 'getting there.' It became obvious what I was doing to myself and I noticed certain patterns. I noticed my nasty habit of wishing my life away. I couldn't wait to be done with school, so I could get to teaching; I couldn't wait to be done teaching, so I could get married; I couldn't wait to get married, so I could have babies; I couldn't wait to end 'this,' so I could start 'that.' This pattern created a blind Abby zipping through a blur I was calling life.

There is a large difference between living a life
that will continuously generate your happiness
and self-worth and struggling through life to get
to some magical point where your happiness lies.

What I determined is that I was never really getting anywhere. I found that life is, and always will be, an ever-evolving process of growth, with milestones of experiences to celebrate along the way. There is no one grand mountain top, and even if I got to one, from there I would see another, and another. It took me two or three mountain tops to realize this. It took getting pummeled by a few falling rocks to be forced to sit long enough to just enjoy the view.

Speaking of learning to enjoy the view, it was on the side of Mammoth Mountain learning to snowboard that I truly quit rushing through life. It was my first time really snowboarding and one of my trailblazing friends,

Jose, took me out on the slopes to shred some gnar—yes, they really say that. He has always been so cool to me, and is the epitome of living in the moment. He has traveled all over the world, and inspired me to take a trip outside of my comfort zone. So here I was, practicing snowboarding, and I had really gotten it down! After he taught me the basics of avoiding face plants and back flips, he headed for the big boy slopes, and I was left to my own devices. I was relieved to go at my own pace, and get a better feel for this whole snowboarding thing. As I made my way down the beginner hills, I was dodging kids and parents out on their family outings, praying I wouldn't roll over the front of their skies. I began to maintain my balance and speed long enough to not take a whopping fall. I was having a blast experiencing learning in the moment and feeling capable again. I forgot what it was like to try new things because I had stopped while I recovered from divorce. Being back in the game of life felt exhilarating.

In the middle of a run, I had stayed upright on my board so long that I was actually tired! Winded and sore, I scooted to the side of the path, sat myself down, and just laughed. I leaned all the way back, sprawled out, stared at the sky, and laughed all by myself in sheer joy. "I am snowboarding, in California. Who am I?" I thought to myself. I just laughed and laughed as I thought about the struggle the last year of my life had been. A year and a week after my husband left me, I was snowboarding in California. A dream I had designated as only a dream had just become my reality. In that very moment, I stopped laughing and started crying. I said to myself out loud, "My problems are nowhere near as big as these mountains. These mountains were here before my problems and will be here after them." In that moment, I had no problems. This is the moment I quit trying to have 'made it.' I quit wishing my life away. I quit convincing myself there was a point in my future where my happiness lies. I began to have my happiness in every moment. I quit waiting for life to show up, and I started showing up to life.

I quit the "Shiny Thing Syndrome." I got home from California and created my second vision board based on the life experiences that I craved. I yanked the 'made it' feeling from the future back into my now. I always sensed my longing for the future, but I thought it meant I was focused and determined. It took realizing that living for the future was stealing my ability to be present, to make a change. I was trying to create experiences of family, fun, and freedom out there, and I had it available right here! I laughed about how I was working both backward and really hard to attain something that was right in front of me. The problem was that I was setting my sights months and years ahead. When I shifted my focus, I began to envision and live out the experiences that filled my soul and life purpose immediately because really, all we have is now. Our past is our past. Our future is uncertain, and all we have is right now, right now, and *right now*. I released my grip on controlling the future and started practicing the same mindset I experienced on the side of Mammoth Mountain. It was then that I began declaring how the rest of my life would go.

Like life itself, success also shape shifts with age. Success is not exactly those shiny things. It is more like living a life that you love. Your fullest vision of success may include shiny things, but it is about experiencing the freedom of full expression of who you are. Success is nailing down your life purpose and living it so boldly that your true essence and impact in the world is undeniable and unstoppable.

The coolest part is, we all have purpose.

Do you know *that* grocery store clerk? The one who knows the regulars by name and always greets you with a genuine excitement? Day in and day out, you can rely on them being there with bells on, and you can't quite understand how they could possibly be so happy being a clerk? We must shift the reality that exists for us and accept that any lifestyle can become a fulfilling one. That clerk is satisfied with themselves and the work they do. It brings them joy and it is an expression of who they are. Whatever it took in their journey, they have crossed many bridges and have found their worth and purpose. They are doing work that brings them joy and fulfillment, because they, themselves are joyful and fulfilled. The line of work doesn't matter. They choose their life from an empowered place.

Yeah, that is what I am talking about! I am talking about the warmth behind the smile of someone with the glorious awareness that there is no one you need to be other than yourself. It is that peaceful understanding that being you is what makes life *so fulfilling*. Lastly, it is the reassurance that being yourself creates the life experience you want to have.

Take some mindful time to consider what experiences you want from life. If you find these questions and points affronting, consider that you have already let go of the possibility that your dreams *can* and *will* come true. The transformed woman who used to be the Jaded Quitter would like to remind you to be kind to yourself. It took quitting a lot of other junk for me to get back to remembering that Life can be whatever you chose, and you are always at choice, my love.

Reflection Questions:

Will the Shiny Things create your everlasting happiness?

What does it look like to just show up as you? (instead of job title, relationship role, or socially acceptable)

What will fill your soul up so much that you decide to show up to life every day on fire?

Do you know and feel your purpose? Are you living it?

What dimensions of your happiness have you cast out into the unpredictable future because you 'just can't have that yet?'

What mountain peak moments have you been chasing?

What climbs have you left unfinished and unfulfilled?

If there was nothing to do and nowhere to be, what would you choose to be doing in life?

Chapter 3

My Unlovable Story

One summer day in therapy, during a full blown Crabby Abby meltdown about my mom, my doctor ever so plainly said, "Wow, you really love your mom, huh?" "Well, YEAH!" I ugly cried back at her. I was doing what kids do where they cry until they start choking and hacking and wrapping it up with the head back, gap-mouthed, silent cry. The sun was shining outside, but the sky was falling in and on my head. During this session, I went on and on about how I wish she were more my friend than my mom. For most of my life, I had felt pretty hopeless about having real, authentic connection with her. I remember envying girls in school whose moms came along on field trips and picked them up from school. I would silently sulk and cling to those moms. It felt so unfair that my mom had to work, and these moms could be here with us. I resented her schedule, and I hated that we only got her on weekends. I also resented our schedule. In her best efforts to give us this great life, we were registered into every sport, club, and activity, then not allowed to quit them. At that phase in life, quality time with Mom was the drive to each basketball game or tournament and her yelling at us to "Box out!" from the stands. I began to hate that weekends were *jam packed* with activities, as opposed to twenty-four seven cuddling, popcorn popping, and movie watching.

Something I remember longing for so desperately was conversation. I remember dying to ask my mom for advice about boys, and help with my homework. I wanted to talk through girl fights and cliques at lunch tables. I was the eldest, so I had no reference for what to do in new situations. I often felt lost in major life transitions like starting middle and high school, and even college. I recall wanting to be able to go to Mom for understanding, guidance, and the occasional hug.

Children are somewhat like animals. They can smell fear. They can also sense bullshit. I have memories that I can draw on in which my mom was clearly overworked, overwhelmed, and overtired. She seemed constantly distracted. There was always a rushed way about her. No time for rest or relaxation for the single mom of two. She seemed to need help and support as much as I did. Being the daughter, I felt helpless in wanting to take her pain or suffering away. I had no idea how to make life better for her other than being perfect, and not causing anything for her to worry about. It didn't eliminate my own needs, but I knew

I wanted to alleviate hers. To no fault of her own, and likely far outside of her awareness, this made me resent the relationship. There seemed to be an imaginary forcefield blocking me from a true, loving connection with my mother, and, as a twelve-year-old, I had no way of identifying or breaking through it. Without understanding this force field, I could only feel and sense it. It was as if this make-believe wall was sound proof, and she couldn't hear me. I became starved for attention. My heart longed for my mom's love and nothing else would do, but she seemed too distracted, and I didn't know how to ask for it. Instead of understanding it, I decided it was the way my mom was, and it felt like I would never be able to connect with her. There was nothing my mom could do right by me at that point. Over the years, I acclimated to this belief and just came to make the most of it. I built my worth around student and athlete, but none of it ever amounted to Mom's love.

So, as I kicked and screamed in this therapy session that all I want is Mom's love and attention, my therapist suggested I just go for it. My quitters were holding both middle fingers up at her because I was feeling like "Lady! Don't you think I thought of that?" To be quite honest though, I hadn't. It dawned on me that I had done just about everything else imaginable other than *just* become her friend. I had achieved amazing things trying to win my mom over, but I had never really considered quitting the charade and just asking her to spend quality, uninterrupted time with me. My anger and tears subsided as we discussed the possibility of me just becoming friends with my mom.

Over the next few months, that is exactly what I did. I never sat her down for a 'come to Jesus' talk, but instead, I invited her to the movies. Then, I accompanied her in her favorite hobby: dog walks. We started going out just the two of us, and I began listening for who my mom was as a woman, instead of just as a mom. I was making a new friend. She was the only friend I had ever wanted my entire life, and now, I had her. I cry as I write this because it means just as much every time I recall 'getting my mom back.' As I once shared with her, I would trade every trophy or medal I ever won for an extra hour of time with her. Restoring my relationship with my mother was the most pivotal phase of my life. I was filled with pure, authentic love because I had taken down the barrier that had always blocked me from her. That barrier was my unlovable story.

I got poked between the eyes by My Unlovable Story during a life coaching exercise. I went to the front of the room at this forum and stood in front of those same hundred and ten people with the intention of getting coached on my career, only to discover that I believed I wasn't worth anything. Even after rebuilding my relationship with my mom, I had some residual self-inflicted pain left over from childhood that I hadn't been able to identify. I had gotten so used to earning love, that to simply receive it wasn't easy at first. I was still pretty convinced that I was unlovable because I had believed it for twenty-eight years. I found that I had memories to sort through that went further back than twelve-year-old Abby. I recalled times in my youth that my mom would come home past my bedtime, and I would secretly stay up in bed to make sure she made it home. I would be overjoyed that she got back after long holiday hours, but equally as disappointed that she did not come in my room to make sure I was there or kiss me goodnight. Although my dad would reassure her that my sister and I were fast asleep, I understood it to mean that when she didn't peek her head in, it was because she didn't care about me. This devastated me as a five-year-old, and I decided right then and there that I was unlovable.

I did not know I had this story running my life until the moment I went up for coaching. I didn't see it as a story, because through time, and my five-year old interpretation, I had turned what had happened into reality. What actually happened was: my parents divorced when I was two. My mom worked sixty or more hours a week to support us financially, and Dad worked for himself on his own time, so we saw more of him during our elementary, middle, and high school years. The five-year-old version of me made up the story that "Mom isn't around as much so she likes work more than me. There must be something wrong with me." I equated that her work must have been more important than me. I convinced myself that I wasn't worth much, or worth being around. So, I began a lifelong battle to win Mom's affection and attention.

A victim lives inside a story. A victim walks, talks, and lives from the perspective of life and tragedy happening *to* them. For as long as I can ever remember, I played the role of neglected daughter who just wanted *all* of Mom's attention. I was in constant competition, on and off the court. It wasn't until I started staring in the self-development mirror that I began to recognize all the ways of being, habits, and beliefs I had developed around this identity. This identity shaped the star student, the perfect angel, the ruthless achiever, and the athlete. This also shaped Crabby Abby who showed up when things didn't go her way. You could watch me all the way through my twenties throwing a full-blown temper tantrum when I felt out of control of a situation or neglected. I would freak out because any time I sensed failure, I believed that my unlovability caused it. As the victim, this was a tragic experience. I was the cause of all my heartache. I would double down on this pattern with self-hate or harsh criticism. This identity shaped every choice from relationships to careers. I was always playing the victim of neglect and rejection. It was the only way I related to the world, and I was *always* trying to fix whatever it was I thought was wrong with me. The real tragedy was that this was my perceived reality for so long.

It is *so* important to say here that there was absolutely no lack of love, and certainly no neglect. It was a five-year-old seeing five percent of a situation. I only had the mental capacity to understand my role in this circumstance, not the entire scope and sequence of my parent's divorce, or the unfolding of our lives from that point forward.

It is likely my mom is laughing, crying, shaking her head, or doing that weird choking noise as she reads this because she doesn't recall that as my childhood. Good, bad, or indifferent, I invite you to recall your version of your childhood to your parents, guardians, or siblings, and hear their memory of your childhood. I am willing to bet it will be laughably different.

As humans, our personal perspectives skew our realities. It is part of human instinct to interpret. This happens all day, every day. We are relating to the world through the filters of our past. It can deceive us into believing crazy things, such that we are unlovable for an eternity, if we do not ever catch it for what it is—a story.

As I was evolving as a life coach, I was being called to higher levels of maturity that I couldn't comprehend. These higher ways of being and acting were not compatible with my unlovable story. Achieving the success I imagined was not possible from my position of 'unlovable,' so I saw road blocks everywhere. That same barrier that I had wedged between my mom and I existed between myself and my success. It required loving myself in order to 'level up' in any area of my life. I was relating to all of life through the unlovable filter, so instead of leveling up, I was falling flat. I could not declare anything possible outside of this filter, and my inner critic certainly had a field day with me during those months of exploration and transformation.

In my last attempt at fixing myself, I took the mic in front of a hundred and ten others and admitted that I had been pretending that I had it all together. I stood there as a twenty-eight-year-old, but the five-year-old who missed her mom was talking. I was pretending I had it all figured out when in fact, I was scared. I was unsure. I knew that I felt unworthy of trust and love, but I was too afraid to show it. I had fears of looking like a fraud, and I had created my identity around hiding those fears. This inauthentic way of being had me living a 'less than' kind of life. I never felt good enough for anything. I was operating in a way that had me feeling fake and stupid. From this way of being, I was missing any sense of freedom, power, fulfillment, authenticity, or connection. The barrier that I had taken down in my relationship with my mom still existed between myself and my self-worth.

So, there I stood, announcing that my goal was to be a life coach, public speaker, and author, with a trembling voice and shaking hands. I announced that I felt selfish for charging people, as if I was stealing money out of their pockets and food out of their mouths. I related to myself as a modern-day thief because I did not feel worth asking for money in exchange for my skills. I had become so used to failing at exchanging my talents for love, that I felt defeated in attempting to make a career out of it. At the mic, I chose to be honest in a way that felt *so* unsafe. I was nervous that admitting my fears would disqualify me from being considered anything near a life coach. I was ashamed of the contradiction I was living, and, as a woman who equated love with worth, I was standing there feeling pretty worthless.

I didn't even grasp it when I was at the mic getting

coached, because at that point, being unlovable was still a fact in my eyes, instead of a story. I had to truly get that I made that up, and it simply wasn't reality. Not until becoming the Enlightened Quitter was I liberated from the life impeding unlovable story. It was the dawn of a new era that granted loads of forgiveness. I let go of the grudge I had against my mom for not kissing me goodnight as that little kid, and I broke through another layer of connection with her. Letting go of that memory that I was using as ammunition against her and myself allowed me to quit working so hard to uphold unlovable, and instead, meet myself for the woman that I am— amazing and worthy of love!

Giving up the unlovable story was like ending a twenty-eight-year drought. I suddenly understood how loved I actually am! Love flooded in because I had removed the dam. It didn't require creating any new love or more hard work. It took releasing my grip on being so right about how 'unlovable' I was, and simply allowing love to reach me. I rebuilt my self-worth out of this breakthrough. I became allowed to own all of my potential. Because of this, I rebuilt the relationship that meant the most to me. I felt worthy of getting hired as a life coach because I came to trust the impact I can create. I began getting more clients, knowing that I deserve them. I have learned that I am making a difference in their lives and this world. Opportunities to collaborate and catch momentum have been laid in front of me.

I began 'leveling up' left and right in life. It didn't require making any crazy shifts in my physical world. I didn't have to be taught what love was. I had to remove the barriers I had subconsciously set up to block it. Once I did this, I kept finding and removing the barriers one by one all over my life. With each one, I fell more in love with myself and more in love with life. I certainly came to believe just how lovable I actually am.

Reflection Questions:

Check out your love language. Your love language is the manner in which you give and receive love. There are five different types and people usually resonate with one or two as their favorites and most impactful. There are quizzes and books out there to find out what you prefer. Find out your peeps' love languages as well. This will create clarity about how you and your significant others prefer to love and be loved. Compare and have yourself a good laugh when you realize that we have love being flung at us from every direction, but we aren't always as open to receiving it as we think or claim. Understanding the five love languages can empower you to share love more powerfully and intentionally.

For instance, I discovered that my love language is quality time, while my mother's is shown through acts of service. As a grown adult, she would come over to clean up my apartment or rearrange it. I never knew what awaited me when I got home, and often couldn't figure out where she had put something. This created guilt and frustration. I didn't hear her speaking love. What I heard was, "You're an incompetent slob and I still need to clean up after your millennial ass." We silently battled in this tug of war for months. I personally struggled with how to solve it. My first response was to ignore it, and therefore, her. I considered asking for my spare key back. I considered calling her and screaming when she would continuously move things and I would have the extra job of putting them back when I got home from work. I was frustrated with the situation of course, but

I was mostly frustrated with the message I thought she was constantly sending. It had to stop, yet, I was at a loss for how to end this without hurt feelings on both ends.

When I learned her love language, all of that changed. I saw how desperately she was trying to share her love and how stubbornly I was rejecting it. It all became clear and I saw how we were both struggling with feeling vastly misunderstood. Understanding her from this new perspective made the steps to ending this battle so clear. I openly acknowledged her efforts to care for me. While I described my frustration, her face showed disappointment in the way I was misinterpreting her form of 'I love you.' I explained to her that I receive love in quality time, and that I would trade every dish she came over to wash for dirtying them over cooking together and having dinner. I told her that her time and attention is the greatest gift she can give me. Together we recreated our love communication, and as a result, have the opportunity to give and receive lots of love in very new ways.

There are a good handful of misunderstandings that can be resolved and recreated by taking the time to understand the other person's intentions. Struggles, arguments, and ongoing battles can be completely dissolved with trained communication and listening skills. I invite you to dig deeper and go one step further in understanding yourself and others. It has been proven effective on a personal, and even global scale. Start with your learning your love language, and then sharing your love in all of your favorite ways.

Chapter 4

My Character

Right in line with my unlovable story, I have been living almost my entire life playing the role of a second-place loser. I like to refer to her as the Honorable Mention Olympian.

The Honorable Mention Olympian plays out a heroic drama that will tie you in, and have you in her corner. All while she plays a strong, independent woman, she is constantly fighting an internal battle of impending doom in which disappointment lurks just around the corner. In this story, she can never have it all. She will always be the one who lost the race by a millisecond. She will have to miss the last shot. She will have disappointed everyone, but mostly, herself. She has learned to live within the underdog role, and loves to do so. It grants permission to fail.

Nonetheless, she will have you tuning in until the very last second. She will keep you at the edge of your seat about an outcome, while the ending defeat is already written. Onlookers helplessly wish more for her. She does not fear defeat, because she has mastered not having to experience suffering alone. She has set herself up to be taken care of by others during her recovery from noble heartbreak.

From this space, she will always be incapable. She will never be able to have it all. Her fullest life is but a dream, and only ever that. A combination of disappointment, loneliness, and despair is her most predictable future. She will always stay small by fighting the little battles instead of conquering the very thing that holds her back: her ego.

Sound familiar? Notice a pattern or theme of being throughout this memoir? What you are noticing is the character I play in life. The Honorable Mention Olympian is my most practiced identity of the victim role. It is the culmination of every quitter I have in my repertoire. She is the biggest quitter there ever was. The ways of being for this character are so automatic that, often times, I don't know she's present until she's running the show, and I am experiencing a total breakdown. By the time I become present, I have already created my newest obstacle in an ensuing battle.

Why tell on myself? Why risk exposing this manipulative character? Why stand face-to-face with potential criticism and rejection? Because I am not that character.

We don't even consciously recognize the character traits that we generate at very young ages until they are shown to us through some phenomenon, or a gracious human. Our brains developed more on certain days, during certain events, that caused us to determine how we would react and what kind of person we would be for the rest of our lives. These character traits have driven us to peaks of success and valleys of disappointment and despair. If we automatically and subconsciously operate from them, they can really control our lives. If we heighten our awareness and decide to choose power-fully, we can be the ones who get to say what life is like. We can actually use our character traits as skills. When we take our life back from our character, it occurs that we happen to life.

Life does not happen to us.

Through very intentional self-awareness, I have seen this character for everything that she is. She is an unlovable, people pleasing, survivor! The more I get to know her, the sooner I see her arriving on the scene. Calling her out for who she is, a real B, grants me access to release her and take my power back. I, Abigail, am the one who gets to say.

I know what I really want my life to look, feel, and be like, so I am taking full responsibility for creating it from the best version of myself—not some character completely shaped by the past, fear, and insecurity. If I wouldn't let a five-year-old drive my car, then I won't let the five-year-old this character derived from run my life.

RIP Honorable Mention Olympian. I've got my eye on you.

Reflection Questions:

If your life were a movie, and you were the main character, what would your character's title be?

If you created a brief synopsis of your character: What are their constant battles and obstacles?

What are their character strengths and shortcomings?

What are the underlying intentions of your character?

If you keep operating as this character, what is your most predictable future?

Chapter 5

My Inner Critic

I had two major breakthroughs in self-hate. The first was with a fellow coach practicing an exercise with me that was meant to grant the participant access to closure, or completion, around a certain person, place, or event in the participant's life. Something I realized while going through my coach certification program was that I had a ton of memories in my life that I did not have closure with. These incomplete events still had a hold on me that required thought and energy. Having so many incompletions in my life left me feeling drained and hollow.

When Jen asked me which area of my life I would like completion, I thought I would use the partnership to go for a big one. I picked college basketball. Holy moley, I know I mentioned basketball was tough, but digging through those memory banks exposed me to how much of that experience shaped my inner critic.

It made clear how much I was still subconsciously holding onto. Going through this conversation made it obvious how much that component of my past contributed to my feeling insufficient, leaving me bruised and bloody.

Dissecting this experience revealed that I was living this past in my present, and would be doing so into my future. Growing up as a student athlete, there is some perfectionism and criticism that seems unavoidable. Coaches often use force, intimidation, and shame as tactics to 'motivate' athletes to never settle and go further, faster. It was a way of being that I applied to most areas of my life, and I submerged myself in the pressure. As a youngster wanting to prove myself, it worked. I was always first in lines, drills, and games. I made sure to work hard enough to be the best. This rocked in high school, but it just barely got me through college. In adulthood, the standard to which I had always held myself was exposed to me as inhumane.

I didn't believe my coaching peers when they said I was being way too tough on myself. After all, I looked up to professional athletes that made a living through this method. There are *plenty* of inspirational quotes to support my belief system! I convinced myself they just didn't get me.

Quite honestly, I didn't want to have feelings about it. I just wanted to be invincible and impeccable. I wanted to be my version of successful, otherwise, I wouldn't attain success. My peers kept loving me by inviting me to 'be kind to myself' and all I could think was, "Oh, yeah, right. As if that's ever gotten me any-where." I was righteous in the worst way.

It feels silly to admit that a meme on Facebook shook my roots. It read: "If being tough on yourself worked, it would have worked by now." Ouch. Ouch, to my ego. Being tough on myself definitely wasn't work-ing. I finally had to take a look at the way I was being about success, hard work, and my humanity, so I agreed to this completion call with Jen.

I did not grasp the real impact of negative self-talk until I heard my own self-loathing words in the context of exercising completion.

Man, I was mean to myself. Hearing this 'athlete' talking about the woman I was working on becoming created such an obvious gap that I had to choose that this self-hate was not going to drive me any further.

From this breakthrough, I took huge strides in cre-ating self-love. I began to tell myself that I was great, even when I didn't believe it. The first few weeks of this was like chewing on tinfoil. I was hating my first swings at self-love. I was so conditioned to beat the ever-living crap out of myself that to just 'be kind to myself' was weird.

The real progress I made came after I realized that self-love isn't cliché like manicures, pedicures, or solo dates to the movie theater. Self-love took shape in the way of caring for myself. I gained a lot of self-love when I stopped trying to do everything alone, and realized it was okay to ask for help and support. Any time I caught myself struggling alone, I considered what my needs were in the moment, and I started meeting my needs. Holy self-love, people. Every time I asked for a hand, life got simpler. I fell more and more in love with myself every time I did this. Team, friends, family, group, and community took on whole new meanings in my life, and I was uplifted.

> My second breakthrough came through
> the acceptance of my humanity.

Reflection Questions:

If being tough on yourself worked, it would have worked by now. How's it going?

As discussed throughout the book, your inner critic is a natural part of the human condition. The chatter never stops. Just because you can hear the chatter doesn't mean that you have to listen to it.

Where and when did you learn to be so tough on yourself?

What phases or events in life turned up the volume on your inner critic's voice?

Consider that your inner critic is a loved one sharing their opinion about how you are living your life. Our loved ones want to keep us safe. Our loved ones want to protect us from this 'harsh world' and yet, we can often relate to them as this harsh world throwing doubt and judgement our way.

Today, you get to practice letting go of the unforgiving conversation constantly going on in the back of your mind. When you hear that negative opinion rising from the chatter, thank your critic for his/her opinion, and let it go. It is just an opinion, nothing more. The chatter you hear holds no validity. It is the opinion of a mechanism meant to keep you comfortable. To have your fullest life, you already know it will require stepping far past the boundaries of comfort. The great news here is that in your journey for your grandest life, you don't have to be the source of all your pressure and criticism. When practiced and used effectively, this will encourage you to go for your dreams boldly, proudly, and with some gosh darn excitement!

Without the negative chatter, in what ways would your mind be freed up to relax and think?

If your mind were clear of chatter, what would you spend your thoughts and focus on?

If you let go of the harsh self-critiquing, what compliments would you pay yourself?

Put this book down for a while and think about how great you are.

Chapter 6

DIY Suffering

I had to have my open wounds shown to me to realize I had them. It required a loving life coach calling me out on how incomplete I was about my childhood and my grudge against Spirit to see the cracks in my trust of Others. In this example, 'Others' represents putting my trust in anything but me.

The Jaded Quitter had collected all the evidence I needed to believe that if I wanted something done right, I'd have to do it myself. She also learned not to get too excited about potential projects or plans. She had plenty of proof that plans fall through. I was always factoring disappointment as part of the plan if it required counting on Others to follow through. Whatever little amount of trust I had dished out, I had secretly begun to take back during my time as the Jaded Quitter. It was an isolating experience to try to succeed alone.

It took breakdown session, after session, after

session, to see that something wasn't working. I had a handful of my coaching colleagues ask me if I was getting support in the form of recovery. After all, it is part of our code of ethics to recognize when someone may be better served by therapy or counseling in order to be properly equipped to create their life powerfully. At this point, I was way too 'strong' to need the help of others. I was still busy trying to be fine after divorce. In my mind, asking for help was at the very bottom of the list for progress and success.

As I have already admitted to you, I wasn't allowing myself to be human, so the idea of taking on therapy didn't seem like the route for me. I had no judgements about therapy itself. I had judgements about who I was, and whether I could handle life myself. Asking for help felt weak to me. I had a parallel relationship with asking for help as I did with quitting in my youth: shame. I was afraid it would mean that I couldn't handle myself. It felt too vulnerable, so I avoided recovery support. The process took many more breakdowns. I found myself devolving for a while in my coach training program. The more I was called forth, the more I reverted to my inner child, throwing temper tantrums and hiding out. I had shifted from trying to move forward to being completely uncoachable. I cannot specifically recall the tipping point, but one afternoon, I found myself in a therapist's office.

Initially, I was struggling with having a failed marriage. I was going through major breakdowns, and I was still trying to get away with living a normal life.

I was determined to escape this event with a clean record. This perceived loss had me cowering, hiding out, and attempting to recover on my own. Any amount of growth I felt came matched with new fear of failure or rejection, because if it happened once, it can happen again, right? I would catch myself 'braced for the impact' of new or different forms of trauma. This had me avoiding full-blown progress and possibility. This was no way to live. Regardless of what strategy I set in place to skirt the hurt, life felt like the moment in movies when the bad guy gets busted, and all the lights and alarms are going off and the cops come rushing to the scene. Total overwhelm and chaos. Of course, I had nowhere to run or hide. I threw my hands up, fell to my knees, and turned myself in. I surrendered the life I was living.

After exploring the inner workings of my independent logic, I could see all of the incompletions from my childhood. Divorce simply tipped the scale on what I could handle with the tools I had. For the first time, I accepted that maybe I wasn't fully equipped to handle this alone. After all, I had never gone through divorce before. I thought it would be like getting over the loss of a loved one, and I had done that. I compared it to a hundred other scenarios, but I had never experienced a setback like this, and the harder I tried, the harder it got, and the harder I pushed myself. I was broken down. First, I got help in the form of therapy, then a dear friend set me up with an inner child specialist, and then I found a support group. I found recovery to be an integral part of creating life powerfully. I like to say to my clients that beginning coaching before they are coachable is like asking them to run a marathon with a ball and chain on their foot. I had to cut my chains before I could jump back in the game of creating my life powerfully.

I had to consciously decide to start choosing to love myself despite my subconscious, and very deeply rooted fears. I began to choose differently. During the recovery process, I stepped *into* and then *out of* suffering repeatedly in order to better understand it. I walked through the chest-burning fires of anxiety to singe off my layers of worry. I sat right there, in a time-out, as I threw temper tantrum after temper tantrum streaming tears of "life's not fair." I touched the stove of self-development time after time to learn "Ouch, that burns" or "Hey, I don't like that."

I stayed in the game of self-development despite the growing pains, and I have learned to absolutely love it. I have learned to absolutely love myself. I learned that I am perfectly fine, and so is everyone and everything. We all have room to grow, but where we are is simply a result of the choices we make and patterns that play out. If we find that we aren't happy with the way it is going, we *can* actually change it!

In many of my writings, I openly talk about raising my little white flag on doing it all alone. I went from not trusting anyone, to being able to rely on others to support me through my struggles, and later, invite them to celebrate with me on the other side of the breakthrough. I was able to distinguish being the One for myself versus struggling alone. I took on being my own advocate in order to maintain momentum with the direction I wanted my life to be going. I can hardly put enough words in this book about enlisting a support structure to move you through your transformation. Nearly every chapter of this book has an example of my calling on a form of support to walk with me through this scary journey.

I invite and encourage you to seek out a more professional form of support if you are seeking an extraordinary life. There is absolutely nothing wrong with an ordinary life. Ordinary lives are great! There can be love, affinity, and joy in an ordinary life, but if you are reading this far, I feel perhaps, that ordinary life is just part of your journey. If you are shooting for an extraordinary life, you will be called to extraordinary levels of being. A really big life calls for a really big you. It will require you at your highest and best. So again, I encourage you to set yourself up with an entourage of empowerment to keep calling you forth out of what is comfortable.

You will gain access to feeling loved, heard, known, and understood. You will feel supported and you will be the one to have created that for yourself. If you give up suffering alone, you may find there is less suffering to do.

Reflection Questions:

Where in life can you use the hand of support?

If you spent a moment to look, do you see memories and events in your life that you could use some assistance recovering from?

What from your past are you holding onto?

If you are like me when I was refusing to ask for help, what judgements to you have about yourself getting support?

What do you say it would mean about you to get help?

If you were to choose to set up a support structure, where would you start?

What would it look like for you to be able to freely move past the things that are holding you back?

What would a life without your suffering be like?

Who would you get to be without all your perceived misery?

Chapter 7

Giving Up Giving Up

When you do enough digging, you hit rock bottom. When you've lifted and sifted every particle of dirt, you'll find yourself at the bottom of a pit, with mounds around you. It's an incredible feeling to be there—indescribable, quite honestly. I'm pretty good at putting words together, but this concept is one you'll have to experience for yourself. May this book be a milestone in your journey to get there.

All I can say is that getting to the bottom of that personal pit was the most enlightening moment of my life. In all of this digging, I thought I would uncover what was wrong with me, but I didn't. I thought I would find a skeleton or a hidden treasure map, but I didn't. I thought I would find the answer, but, again, I didn't. I found nothing, really. I found myself sitting at the rock bottom of my emotional pit. To get to the bottom, to finally hit a destination and realize that there is absolutely nothing to do there, was simply jaw dropping. There's no more digging. There's no more fixing. There's no nothing, and if you sit there down long enough, it'll really sink in. There is nothing to do but be. Be *with* everything that you are and everything you are not. Be with your essence. Be with your survival mechanisms. Be with your greatness. Be all of it, and understand that this is who you are.

Sit and stay awhile in order to truly learn yourself. If you submerge yourself in the pit long enough, you will go through all the stages of transformation. You will come to identify who you are and how you survive. You will come to know who you truly are, past your fears and doubts, and come to accept the highest and best version of yourself. To come to accept, and even own yourself, finally gives you access to self-love! This is the exciting part, because the moment you do it is the moment you start climbing right out of that pit, ready to go be yourself with the world! Who you are is going to change this world. You absolutely must unleash it. The world is waiting for you to show up at your highest and best.

My Quitters still exist. My desire to please is constant. My craving to be liked is insatiable. The difference is those quitters and characteristics are no longer running my life without my knowledge. I have stepped into my power and I have taken my life back. I have pushed far past the imaginary barriers that I lived inside of to create a life I could only speak about two years ago. Because I took back my Power, I have been empowered to live a life I love.

Reflection Questions:

If I told you that there is nothing wrong with you, how inclined would you be to believe me?

If I threw you into the bottom of your pit, what fears would you face?

If you are reading this book to find out or fix what's wrong with you, read it again, and again, and again, until you get that all there is to do with you is to learn, own, love, and be you.

Part Four

Accepting and Choosing

Chapter 1

Who I Am
and Who I Am Not

One day, I was given a completion exercise to call some-one and 'get complete' with them. This meant picking up the phone and saying whatever I needed to say in order to be authentic and feel fully expressed with that person. I chose my mom. I have shared that we had already moved mountains in our relationship, so I was calling to really feel complete with this amazing trans-formation we had made.

Now, I would consider myself a very expressive woman. I have always been very sensitive and emo-tional. I love sharing my feelings with others, but when it comes to my mom, I always brace myself for how she might respond. In my eyes, she can tend to be a real no-nonsense type of woman. So, with a racing heart and slight panic in the back of my mind, I dialed my mom. There is usually about a six percent chance of her being available, but she picked up! I blame the build-up of anticipation, but immediately, I start with a rush of sniffles and tears, "Hi Momma, I'm at a coaching forum, and they invited us to call someone that we want to share ourselves with. I wanted to call you and tell you how much I love you! I am so glad that we have grown together over the past few months, and I am beyond grateful to have you in my life as a friend and Mom. It just means so much to me!" I type this as a cohesive sentence, but there was that weird coughing, choking, and hacking happening between every other word.

She nearly cut me off in my sobbing declaration of love as she blurted out back at me, "Abby, are you on your period!?!"

"No, Mom!" I whined back at her, and I almost reverted back to that twelve-year-old. Crabby Abby was creeping up. I took a deep breath and responded from what I had discovered about myself, "I have always been an emotional person, and I just never expressed it toward you because you react like that! I never felt allowed to be emotional around you, but this is who I am, and I want you to know how much I love you!" There was silence on the other end. For a second, I was sure she had hung up. I even pulled my phone away from my head just to make sure she didn't. "Ya know," she sighed, "we think we are doing our best for the ones we love, and it never quite turns out the way we think," she replied in a soft, loving tone. "I love you too, Abigail."

We talked for another minute and said our goodbyes.

Her response in that phone call truly completed a lifetime of struggle I had created between us. My Mother, THE Deb, has always done her best to give her daughters a good life. She has always used the tools and skills she has to express love the only ways she knows how. As I had discovered when I learned love languages, I had to take responsibility for, and adjust my perception of her, to see her sharing her love. I had to adjust my relationship to her in order to receive her love. I use my words to express myself and my love. She tends to express her love with gifts or acts of service. I considered her wrong for being that way throughout my life. I made it mean she wasn't emotional, and I couldn't connect with her. I missed out on a lot of love because, to me, her expression of love wasn't compatible with mine. Learning to see this reminded me that everything is just fine. This gave me another opportunity to love her for who she is and who she is not. It was also an opportunity for me to further accept exactly who I am, and who I am not.

There was an epiphany I had at the bottom of that emotional pit I had spent so much time digging for myself. I had cycled through my stages of quitterdom until there was nothing left for me to do but surrender. I could no longer fight against the obstacles I had disproved. I became present to the fact that I have no barriers to my success unless I create them. I have no more excuses. I ran out of hang-ups to keep me snagged up in my woes. It was simply my time to be responsible for the life I want. It was time to go for it.

Sometimes when I noticed this, I would create new problems to have just to stay safely wrapped up in my comfort zone. My subconscious would get ahold of me and make me think I couldn't reach the level of success I dreamed of so fondly. This trick didn't last long. I now knew those were my quitters telling me to run. It was my ego wanting to look good and my insecurities trying to hide out from looking bad. Unfortunately for my ego, I had created too much accountability for myself to return to any ordinary life. With the support of my life coach colleagues, I was encouraged to choose my life from the highest and best version of myself. I knew I was up for a bigger game, so I sought transformation until there was nothing left to do but accept my greatness, and create my life out of it.

I had previously done everything imaginable to generate love from outside sources. The biggest breakthrough about this way of being stemmed from the part that frustrated me the most; the feeling of accomplishment never lasted long. When others were my primary source of love, the feeling and the high went away when they did. The victory faded as soon as I left the court. The pats on the back stopped after the awards ceremony. The applauses lulled after the performance, and there I was, left in silence and longing for more. It was never enough when it came from others. When I realized how temporary this surface level feeling of achievement was, I decided it was time to find a new source to generate my worth.

It was finally time to be my own parent, lover, and

friend. It was up to me to be what I needed in the world. I would be the one to meet my needs or speak them in such a way that others would meet them for me. It was simply time to be my own source of fulfillment and love. In my quitting, I discovered that I do not belong to anybody nor did anyone belong to me. There was fear in this initial discovery, but then there was freedom. It was time to truly create my life by myself and for myself. Once I figured this out, I was set free to create life according to Abigail. Starting with myself allowed me to get back to creating in the world. Only this time, I was truly creating from my heart. Instead of being someone others were sure to approve of, I became someone that I approve of.

Accepting this mission set the stage for full throttle transformation. It created the clarity in my mind that bulldozed a path for me to follow. That path had been there my entire life. It's the one that you seek, but is covered by brush and overgrowth. It is the trail that you recognize as soon as you see it. Seeing it, even for the first time, makes turning onto it feel so natural, and once you do, there's no looking back. Finally hitting the turn finally feels right. It fits. Once I saw the path that had been available to me for so long, I took it. I took it, and there I went. Never to return.

Well, let me rephrase that whole 'never to return' thing. There have been days that I wished to return to my old life. I would catch myself wishing my husband never left me. I wished I got to have that house with those babies and that teaching job. There were tough days in my new expedition where my simpler life seemed, well, simpler. I wrestled with that 'grass is greener' feeling every time my new ventures got big and scary. I would wallow in turmoil about what the future holds for me. Sometimes I would convince myself that my past wasn't as bad as I thought. I fantasized about going back to my old, predictable routines. I romanticized my past in a way that had me thinking, "Well, now, that wasn't *that* bad!" and so I would wish my past back.

In the journey of transformation, with the support of powerful questioning and reflection, there are a few phases that, once you have broken through, you simply cannot *truly* go back. You cannot unlearn yourself once you stand in the mirror of transformation. You cannot unhear your own words, and you cannot deny your heart's desires. You can certainly try, but that little voice inside your head will grow much louder and more powerful over you. Once you have taken a stand not to live from your old ways of being, they become so evident that your choices become clear: go back to surviving or choose to thrive. When I quit everything, everything became clear to me. I had been fitting Abby into the roles of job titles and descriptions my whole life. I was trying to fit into a static way of being, and it left no room for the dynamic Abigail I knew to show up. The more I tried, the more obvious it became. I was surviving.

To *finally* accept that I do not fit in anyone's boxes set me free to be me. Meeting myself outside of any identity revealed my truest passions! Quieting that inner critic and chatter of the outside world hushed my mind in such a way that my heart got a chance to speak up. This has occurred periodically throughout my life, but the major difference was that I was ready and willing to listen. I chose to thrive.

My gut had been telling me that I want to make a difference all along. I *love* public speaking. I *love* inspiring others. I *love* sharing insight in such a way that others consider that there is a whole world of possibility available at all times. It took believing it for myself to be able to share it with others. This would have never been possible had I not shed the weight of my quitters.

In this wave of revelation, I have come to accept me. In shedding the weight of who I am not, I have further accepted all that I am. I have come to accept my passions, interests, talents, and vitality. I have come to love my sensitivity and connectedness. I smile knowing that I can make a difference because now I don't just live *to* inspire. I *live* inspired. I live as a walking, talking example of going for the life you love and living it powerfully. I love who I am, and I love inviting others to find out who they are.

Chapter 2

My Humanity

My second breakthrough in self-love was a real tear-jerker for me. I was sitting in a new, ontological forum, when the leader of the room held up her finger and explained the physicalness of reality. She bent her finger to display everything in reality being an agreement with each other. "The desk is in the agreement with the floor that it will not go through it. We are agreement with walls that we cannot walk through them," she said, still holding her finger in the air.

To display the physical relatedness, she then bent her finger forward so the air around her finger moved. It may be considered just one tiny movement, but in that conversation, I saw the air from the front of her finger pushed forward in its path all the way around the earth and back around to the back of her finger. I attached my inner dialogue to the movement of her finger. "I'm a piece of shit," I said internally as I watched her finger move, "I'm a piece of shit. I'm a piece of shit. I'm a piece of shit." I said it as many times as her finger moved. It sunk in more with each repetition. This was what my inner critic would say multiple times a day when I sensed disappointment and failure. I understood every negative experience to mean that I was the cause of it going wrong. If my actions were not aligned with my intentions, the internal beating would ensue. It had been constant for a large portion of my life, but I hadn't completely identified its impact until this moment. I had to sit there and mourn the fact that I, myself, create my identity, and if I perpetuate the idea that "I am piece of shit," I am in fact going to be just that. It doesn't matter how anyone else in the world relates to me. If I believe I am the scum of the earth then that is the limit to which my potential will be reached. This self-fulfilling prophecy would continue to be a part of any relationship, project, success, or failure I have. It would require choosing a new identity to step outside of the "I'm a piece of shit" cycle and into self-love.

An interesting thing about the reality of our words, is that we choose them. We create them and we perpetuate them. Our word represents us. What happened shows up in facts and figures. Our interpretations of the past are what create our stories, so I decided to end my story about being a piece of shit. What happened in the past fueled my belief about being a failure. I thought about all the phases in my life and number of times per day I would tell myself that. Whenever I would sense failure or disappointment, it was like clockwork that my internal dialogue would turn up the volume to remind me of what a piece of shit I am. It occurred as if there was failure in my life because of this fact about me.

To see it for what it is alone can be so motivating that you want to never choose it again. This belief system was toxic to my sanity and possibility. For a while, I stopped chasing my dreams because of this belief. Seeing how much of my life I had wasted believing something that isn't true changed my perspective in an instant. I can choose that I am wonderful. I can choose that I am perfect, whole, and complete. I can choose to be loved in all areas of my life. I can choose something, anything, other than just being a piece of shit.

Giving up this last story not only put an end to a crappy cycle, but it completely unleashed me to go for my full potential. Noticing the impact of my negative self-talk, I very intentionally shifted my internal dialogue to a conversation around how capable I am. I started rooting for myself, giving myself pep talks, and inspiring myself to take action in achieving my dreams. And you guessed it, since I was struggling with this new way of being, I called in the troops. I both know, and can regularly access the second best way to experience self-love; my team. On any given day, I know who I can call to remind me of who I am, and to get back to being me.

Accepting my humanity has set me free. It has required self-love that I originally did not have the capacity for. For me, accepting my humanity looked like letting go of perfection and accepting progress. Becoming human meant accepting that I have needs and feelings, and that being human is okay. I had to actually surrender and trust others. This took a ton of practice and a lot of shoulders leaned on. A beautiful byproduct of accepting my humanity was accepting the humanity of others. I gained full access to the hearts of others that I had been so desperately seeking as the Subtle Quitter. Becoming human has been an uncomfortable challenge, but a rewarding one. Becoming human has been my greatest adventure.

Reflection Questions:

What sort of internal dialogue do you notice is on repeat?

When disappointment or failure come creeping up, what occurs within you?

What external patterns play out with this internal dialogue?

In what areas of your life do you most experience yourself not being allowed to be human?

What would have to happen for you to let go of this self-criticism?

What would you rather create to be true about you?

Chapter 3

My Big Ol' Heart

This one goes out to my serial monogamists! This chapter is for those of you who are in long-term relationships one after the other. Even after one ends, you find another one, and create something new and fresh from it. It's important that you understand that I'm not addressing anything that's wrong with us. In fact, quite the opposite, I am celebrating what's right with us! We have so much love in our hearts that a relationship seems like the most sensible place to apply it. I considered myself a serial monogamist because I had been in a series of relationships from my sophomore year of high school all the way through being married. I would only be single long enough to find the next significant other. This factored out to about twelve years of relationships with a month or two gap in between each. It never occurred to me as something wrong at all. Still doesn't.

In the pits of my transformation, I saw something that hadn't been so obvious before. While a relationship was easy for me to create, I was simply making up for the love and attention I felt I was missing from Mom. I was stuffing the Mom void with the love of a man. If I had a break up, finding a new relationship was much easier than dealing with the underlying fears and feelings that would surface after a month or two. My unlovable story would confuse me. I would feel lonely or even bored. Being in a relationship calmed my nerves and quieted the chatter. I would validate my lovability by getting a boyfriend. It would alleviate my anxiety. I was dating to feed love to an insatiable heart. I was dating to resolve the unlovable story that I didn't know I had about myself. Talk about a recipe for confusion.

Before I understood it all, my relationship with how much love and attention I required was a disempowering one. I felt *so needy,* but I covered it up with an independent persona. I would crave admiration so badly that I would go to amazing lengths to get it. I noticed that I would take on a new relationship when I really didn't need one. I would date guys that I wasn't very compatible with. I spent so much time tolerating relationships that would have been more beneficial to end. I saw how I compromised my priorities to feel the calmness and comfort a relationship provided me. When I saw this pattern, I swore myself single. It occurred to me that I was using relationships like a drug. If I was feeling low, worthless, or lonely, I would immediately seek out attention. In my eyes, the safest, most reputable form of this was a relationship. Seeing the source of this cycle, what I now jokingly call my "mommy issues," has allowed me to go to Mom when I need her love instead of working backwards to feel the presence of love in my life. Something that this cycle blocked was getting to know myself and blossom as the source of my own love. Only spending a month or two being single prevented me from having my own identity breakthroughs earlier in life, because I was occupying myself with the identity of girlfriend.

Now, back to the whole 'serial monogamist' concept! I'm celebrating the immense amount of passion and love we have! My negative relationship to how much love I have switched in one single acknowledgement from a life coach of mine, during a very tough phone conversation. I was spending the whole call beating myself up for the extreme level that I feel I care, and in contrast, how little I felt I was making an impact with my caring. It was an all talk, no walk kind of feeling. I was griping about having a heart bursting with so much love it hurt. The level at which I felt I cared was not equivalent to the difference I was making in any area of my life. I felt like it was working against me and my mission. I remember judging myself for how strongly I would feel everything. I took everything so personally and I saw everything as a threat to my emotions. I thought I was some type of manic.

I was letting my inner critic speak out loud and tear me apart for having all of these feelings. Mind you, this was far before I accepted my humanity. So, I am going on and on with my woes when Lindi stopped me. She took me out of my self-hate long enough to acknowledge me for my insanely passionate love. She called it 'volcanic.' The very moment that I heard 'volcanic love' was the most self-acceptance I had ever felt to date. In that instant, I stopped fighting it. I completely accepted the amount of love that I have, and this volcano erupted! I learned that it doesn't require getting into a committed relationship to create love! My focus shifted to the love that is already present in my life. I nurtured the relationships that I already had and began to create so much newness! I opened up new pipelines of love in every direction. I saw how love can show up in the world a million different ways. I realized that I can thrive and flourish in every way imaginable, and I let go of thinking that a relationship is the only way to give and receive love. Instead, I began creating it everywhere. Love became an expression of me, not something that I do or create.

Consider a person born with musical inclinations, they have music in their heart, mind, and soul. Musicians find a way to use instruments of all sorts as vessels to create from their true essence. We, as lovers, feel the strength of our natural inclination to love. From this breakthrough, I built a new relationship with connection. I am now free from needing a romantic relationship simply to create closeness, and I can openly use my love to thrive and flourish from it.

I have come to enjoy the natural gift that I have. I have learned that I can use it in every area of life, and have it create more connection and beauty in the world. I have taken crazy, awesome action to share all of this love, and because of it, my life has flourished! Once I stopped resisting it, I was able to realize exactly how abundant my love is. I feel like this heart can generate enough energy to light the city of New York! There is love swirling everywhere! I'm not perfect at it, and I am certainly learning the ropes, but I can tell you that it's much more enjoyable than trying to contain it.

Reflection Questions:

Would you consider yourself a serial monogamist??

Have you stayed in a specific series of relationships as a fix for a story you have about yourself?

What are your gaps and voids in the area of love and what are you filling them with?

What is your most valued source of love?

Do you ever find yourself struggling with the amount of love you feel in your heart? In what ways are you applying it in your life and the world?

Could it be possible for you to channel your amount of love, harness it, and unleash it in a way that serves your bigger 'what for?'

What would it look like for you to use your love outside of relationship?

Chapter 4

My Gift

As a kid, I wasn't too sure about the gift that I was. I knew I was talented, but I blamed that on my competitive nature. I knew I was smart, but I credited that to wanting approval of teachers and parents. I knew I was beautiful…sort of…sometimes…in the right lighting. No matter what I understood intellectually, I didn't really own it. I thought that to own your brain, brawn, and beauty was arrogant. I wanted to be liked and loved, so I attempted to stay humble with my words and let my actions do the talking. After all, who wants to hang around with an arrogant know-it-all, anyway? I would do my best at contributing, while putting on that I didn't think I was that great. It was a very inauthentic and confusing way of being. It was fake, and instead, caused me to seem frustrated or impatient.

I learned that my effort to look humble was a desperate shot at being accepted by others. To make matters worse, my facade of humility was undermined by the fact that I outperformed people constantly. I had collected proof of this as early as sixth-grade basketball when I was called a 'ball hog' for the first time. I was a head taller than everyone else and knew the game already. I would get frustrated with the bopping around, so I would take the ball and go score. It seemed basic to me, and I thought my team would love winning, but it never occurred to me that they were on the court to play, not necessarily to win. This was the first time I thought my athletic attributes weren't attributes and that maybe, just maybe, I was a nuisance. I took it personally and in some ways, I capped my greatness. I toned it down when I thought it would get me rejected, and my belief that I shouldn't fully unleash my greatness began early on in life. Secretly, I could tell I was skilled. I could sense that I was pretty darn good at a lot of things, but it didn't serve my relationships to go off proving my skills to everyone.

I was raised on dirt bikes, roller blades, and skateboards. My dad had us climbing trees and lighting campfires at age eight or so. Both of my parents were into construction, so I could lay concrete and hammer a nail as well as the guys working for my dad. My mom let us help remodel the house, so my sister and I were skilled at working with tools. Our treat for helping lug wheel barrels was practicing driving the pick-up truck at the city dump, so I could even drive ages before my peers. I felt like being born from my parents made me a well-rounded athlete by nature. It never occurred to me as anything different, besides being awesome to have such cool opportunities from such a young age. As a middle and high schooler, I dominated courts and fields and loved it. It was a place where I felt comfortable, and of course, I could usually control the outcome, so that is what I defaulted to. This was seen by peers as either leadership or arrogance and selfishness. It teeter-tottered constantly. I became overly nice to sway my peers to play with me instead of against me, and it worked, for the most part.

Unfortunately, it took me until my young adult years to learn that you simply cannot please everyone, so back then, I still tried to. A great childhood friend helped me reach closure about these memories just a few months ago. You can bet it was another completion call during which she said to me, "Abby, no matter if you screwed it up in your attempts, everyone always knew you were coming from the heart." Her statement left me so complete that I could die any day knowing that people get that about me. I never mean harm. I may make a hot mess of situations sometimes, but it is never out of malice or spite. I am glad to know this now, but I sure spent a lot of time feeling judged and disliked by others in my youth.

This whole 'don't be too great' thing followed me through college and into teaching. People may have thought I was an achiever but I was often operating at about eighty-percent capacity. I was always telling myself that I am 'too much' for people. Too passionate, too committed, too emotional, too everything! I tried to keep the hundred percent Abigail under control unless I felt safe to be her. I think that is why I found such solace in education. I reasoned that teachers were caring people, and it seemed like an arena in which I could be all of me. This proved untrue as time went on. I found that even the halls could be a danger zone for being a complete rock star. It hit me like a brick the day I was called a 'brown-noser' as a teacher, by a teacher. I kept score of every single time I got dinged for going above or beyond what was expected of me, and there were a lot of those moments.

I felt a huge rift in my life. I felt vastly misunderstood. Now, I have come to acknowledge my personal commitment to excellence. I love doing great work. I believe in things being done to their best, but the impression I was creating was 'perfectionist.' For a while, I just gave up fighting it and became one. It was what I was sure others were saying about me. So, I made up the story that I am a perfectionist, a control-freak. I drew the line, stepped over it, and walked it for most of my young adult years, but I knew this wasn't me. I had become so rigid. I was easily irritated when things didn't go as planned. It was exhausting to hang on to this persona, and she was sucking all the joy out of my life. I would ask the extra question in class. I would go the extra mile on a project or goal, or I would literally run the extra mile in sports. This felt good when it worked in my favor, but it stung like hell when I got criticized for it, and it wasn't winning me any meaningful relationships. I translated each negative response to mean I was lame or a loser. My quitter *loved* to run from these situations.

I would run to a safer circumstance. I could only wait to graduate away from it in school, but the switch from teaching to management was great. Rule followers are loved in management…by upper management. I found out all too soon that management was disliked by anyone they enforce the rules on. I remember gagging about showing up at work where I perceived that everyone hated me for being this uptight rule follower. I hated that what I viewed as an asset, others despised me for. Sprinkle on my divorce, and this experience became unbearable. I couldn't stand it. My fear of rejection won this round. Facing that fear never got more comfortable, so I quit.

I ran into the loving arms of a network marketing company, where you get to be your own boss, and praised for overachieving. You get showered with gifts and trips for being dedicated, passionate, persistent, and determined. I felt like I had found the promised land. I had found my niche, and it worked! I got promoted quickly and swiftly.

This is also where my strategy lost its power, of course. I became so addicted to the praise that I worked my face off. The money was just a bonus. The praise was like gold. I got distracted by this abundant availability of love and hit a euphoric state. I worked so hard day in and day out that I forgot what I was working for; more time at home and with my husband. I was setting myself up to be a stay at home mom, but at the rate I was working, I wouldn't have found myself home much at all. I was doing that white-lightening-blur level of motion and commotion in my life.

So, the day Johnny asked for a divorce, I was stopped dead in my tracks. It was almost like blowing a fuse. I had gone into overdrive with achieving, over heated, and had a complete meltdown. Divorce made me so incredibly raw to rejection that even the thought of asking a bathroom attendant for toilet paper seemed risky! I attempted to proceed with my direct sales business as usual, but a switch was flipped in me. I was fearful, hesitant, defeated, and flat-out scared. The characteristics that had made me successful my whole life were no longer effective. I quit my business at the peak of its production. I vividly remember one rainy day in June. I was on the phone with my network marketing sponsor, and she was trying to support me through this hit I had just taken. She reminded me that I would bounce back emotionally and that things would pan out. I remember crying as hard as it was raining. I admitted to her that I simply couldn't handle one more "no." She lovingly reminded me that she would always be available, and that taking care of myself is always the priority. We said our goodbyes, and I hung up and cried some more. I thought this was going to be my life path, and it seemed to be my pitfall. I stopped cold turkey at growing my biz and my team. I withdrew and remained in the fetal position, protecting my heart for the next few months.

If I had any previous hesitations that it was unsafe

to be me, there was absolutely no more questioning that being me was a sure fail. I was far too hurt to learn any lessons at this time, so it required some tears and days strung together watching *Friends* with the shades drawn before I was ready to start showing back up to life. I had to recover before I could get back into any games I had previously been playing. So, I did. I put an 'I'm okay' mask on and tip-toed through life desperately needing to be cared for and loved.

It took therapy to meet the Abigail I knew once upon a time. I met more of the Tired Quitter in therapy. I understood that I was compromising my authentic self for all the praise from wherever I could get it. My insatiable need for validation led me to my doom. This became the single hardest lesson I learned when I was forced to give it all up and become me again. I accepted this lesson with all of its bumps and bruises because to deny it would have meant squandering all it took to learn it. I accepted my divorce with grace and gratitude. I understood that I got a second chance at life and real love. So, instead of spending another minute wallowing, I got into action about meeting me again.

Becoming myself again proved as exciting as it was scary. I understood that I would not truly be meeting old Abby. I am a new person with way more experience. There was really no such thing as simply going back. I took responsibility for who I wanted to become. One day, in my life coaching program, I was asked if I was ready leave that girl behind to become a woman. I stood there, caught off guard. I had never been asked a question like that. I envisioned myself at a fork in the road. I was staring off to my left down a very predictable path littered with jerseys, trophies, beer bottles, and lined with cute boys. I looked to my right and saw a big, brick wall. I had not the slightest idea what Abigail looked like as a woman, but in that moment, I chose the wall. I had no clue what was on the other side, but I went sprinting at it full steam ahead, and I tore that damn thing down brick by ever loving brick.

I didn't *find* woman Abigail, I built her. I used those bricks to build a Powerhouse of a Woman. I still add bricks to my being, but now I know that I am the one who gets to say what the floorplan looks like. I have learned to love this project and accept that it will always be a work in progress. I construct additions as I go to support how much larger I am growing.

As I have grown as a woman, so has my leadership. My old, approval-seeking way of being had limited others around me in the past because I didn't have the skills to lift others up with me. Because personal praise was my driving factor, I became used to being a lone leader. I could teach almost anyone anything, but it being all about me was a huge gap in my leadership that created a quicksand feeling in the success department.

As I took on the work of ontological coaching, I could no longer get away with that funny business. After all, I was being trained to be a life coach and leader. I took on a career in making other people successful. Considering that ontology is the study of the nature of being, I could NOT get away with being anything but authentic. Leaders and colleagues in this work began to call me out on my greatness. This was a totally new brand of greatness, mind you. I tried the winning strategies I had used my whole life, and they called me out on my BS faster than fast. They called for the genuine heart I have and the unlimited potential that they could see in me. One of my favorite things about a rigorously trained coach is that they can hear past what you are saying. They can listen in between your words for what you really want. I wanted freedom. I wanted to unleash all of my power unapologetically, but I wanted permission. I had convinced myself that it was emotionally unsafe to fully be me, so I capped myself everywhere. My coaches and colleagues were sure to point out the limits I had set for myself.

They saw me as my highest and best self and never, ever let me off the hook in becoming her. My frustration with their intention to have me be the best version of myself further exposed that I was dimming my light for fear of being disliked. I convinced myself that I can, in fact, be too awesome, and that it is offensive to others. Based on the evidence I had collected, it was unsafe to be *all* of my greatness. In my past ways of being, it meant that I would leave others feeling 'less than.' I translated it to mean that others would think I was better than them and not want to be around me. This idea used to scare the hell out of me, and it was the last thing I wanted. Since I had collected all of this proof from my past, I projected it into my future.

I was naturally forced to surrender those beliefs

when I saw them holding me back from living my fullest life. Being coached and being a coach requires an incredible amount of boldness and bravery, and thank sweet baby Jesus it does! In the beginning, I was trying to stay humble when asking for my full coaching rate, and it created an insecurity in me that I wasn't worth the dollar amount. It also blocked me from understanding the magical difference that coaching makes. To protect myself, I pretended I wasn't sure what I was doing, and it prevented me from trusting and loving myself. I had spent twelve months training to become an ontological life coach and was practicing and learning more every day. I had all the tools, skills, and resources available, but I wasn't breaking through. As a result, I stayed safe, and saw very little progress.

My world got rocked when someone shared the greatest lesson that I have learned about life: "You don't win unless everyone else wins."

This rule had me take a much closer look at my leadership. I had to have a really good cry when I realized how I was limiting others. I wanted them to be great, but not greater than me. I realized that I had been operating with a fear of being left behind and forgotten. I was afraid that if people were greater than me, I would lose my value to them. This had me subconsciously withholding from giving all of my love in order to be a positive force and leader in this world.

Once I released the fear of being forgotten, I

grabbed onto my greatness. I quit the small game of being accepted, and chose the bigger picture of making a difference, instead. I accepted the innate, intuitive skills that I have. I starting taking risks, without allowing the crippling fear of rejection. I walked all the way up to the edge of that fear at each opportunity I had. I would say what needed to be said in order to authentically support others in their journey. At times it felt scary to unveil to others their own patterns that were holding them back, but I began to own what felt natural to me, and trust where my heart was taking me. I started to make sure that everyone was winning the game they wanted to be playing. As a result, I experienced myself as bold and brave. I was listening for what meant most to people and reliably delivering what would serve and support them in winning their game of life. I became the one holding people accountable in being the greatest version of themselves, the way my peers had done for me! I was calling people forth to shine brighter and bolder! Above all, I was finally experiencing myself as a life-transforming coach, and a completely badass one at that! It was the gift that set me free to be my greatness. I granted myself permission to be amazing, and I have been unleashed.

Learning that rule of life has truly been the best gift I have ever received. Right then and there, I came to understand the gift that I am, and I began to share it. In fact, I couldn't share it fast enough. I couldn't unleash others' greatness fast enough! I have taken on bigger and bigger projects to reach more and more hearts. This book is born from that passion. My life's work has been born from this passion.

There really is no greater gift than simply living as yourself. There is no higher calling than being bold enough to be yourself. It is apparent when someone is truly being themselves. Their Soul shines. The essence of who they are becomes obvious. Souls are so powerful and beautiful when they are the highest and best version of themselves.

We become our highest and best when we accept our greatness and the call to share it. Our calling is to accept our passions and natural gifts, and use them to transform this world for the better. In practicing this, I have accepted the gift that I am, and I shine as brightly as possible. I have accepted the opportunity to be a beacon of light for others. I want to shine a light on others' possibility so brightly that they are drawn to their own greatness, as though a gravitational pull has a hold of them. I connect to the hearts of others by being connected to my own. My goal has become to unleash the hearts of this world so that the ripple effect of hundreds of thousands and millions will generate a wave of greatness that cannot be avoided. Eventually, everyone will get swallowed up in a tidal wave of love and affinity.

You'd be fooling yourself not to own and share your greatness. You'd be selling yourself very short your whole life to stay at a job you hate, or a place you don't like. Your only job on this planet is to get to know yourself so well, that your gift and purpose becomes obvious to the point that you cannot ignore it. If your heart is being pulled in a direction, trust it. If your gut is in knots because you're not following it, face the fear and go past it. If you are completely terrified to go past the fear and into the unknown, get a coach. Seriously, I would NOT have gone this far without a support structure and accountability along the way. If you are serious about having the life you dream about, a coach will walk side by side with you along the way.

You are meant for more. It is your responsibility to heal any wounds so that you may go into your quest whole and complete. If you need help healing, get a therapist. Join a support group. Call a hotline. There are online resources for free, as well. It is the twenty-first century for crying out loud! Getting support is both available and affordable. Forget about any stigmas, and ask for a hand. Support is on the other end of asking for it. It is up to you to take action, because no matter how much we are hurting, others may not be able to see it. It is up to us to get the help we need. Get into contact with professionals who can get you set up for success. It is your responsibility to develop yourself firmly enough to stand in the face of any obstacle as you carry out your mission to make this world a great one. Getting support in doing so is a form of power and strength, not weakness or fragility.

I invite you to consider yourself operating at maximum capacity. Envision having it all. Whatever that looks like for you, I invite you to dream again. I dare you to dream even bigger than that, love. Imagine the world we would create if our jobs were to leave a legacy of love, kindness, compassion, forgiveness, expression, celebration, and joy. Your job is to live a life you love and be an example that it is possible. Your loving yourself will serve as hope to others that they can, too. Your gifts are unparalleled. There is no one exactly like you. This world needs you. It needs your ideas and passion. Go for it and execute that job so well that quitting would be laughable, and walking away would never truly be an option again.

So, I challenge! I challenge you to quit. I challenge you to quit trying to fit yourself into some box that feels comfortable. Accept your greatness, and blow the lid off of your possibility!

Reflection Questions:

Are you present to the true gift that you are?

Do you have your own permission to be the gift that you are?

What evidence have you collected throughout your life to conclude that it isn't safe to be the most authentic version of yourself?

What barriers have you set up to protect your heart from the fear of criticism or rejection?

What are you missing out on by capping your greatness?
What does a fully unleashed you look like??

What kind of life would you create with permission to be your greatest self?

Make a list of the gifts that you have and the gift that you are.

Chapter 5

My Purpose

As we grow our practices as life coaches, we are often asked who our clients are. We are encouraged to find a niche market that we are interested in serving, and this is what I had the hardest time with. "Uh, everyone!" I would mentally respond in my snottiest way. I am sure I wore my response on my face, or the eye roll gave it away. It felt criminal to leave anyone out. I want everyone to have their best life. It seemed too selective or privileged for me to be the one to decide, so I stayed open. I ask anyone I can work up the guts to ask if they are interested in receiving coaching.

I was largely the Jaded Quitter when I was starting my new career, so going out and asking everyone proved ineffective. It was like the Jaded Quitter was out to prove a point that *no one* wanted coaching, and here I was, fantasizing that I was going to save the world with my newly chosen career path. My character I play in life, Honorable Mention Olympian, loved this struggle. I was up against an obstacle to overcome, but I knew better, I didn't want to be this character in life anymore. I wanted to be an impactful woman and coach. Instead, I became afraid of rejection in my first few months of growing as a coach. We were asked about our target market month after month, and the more swings I took at getting clients, the more I understood the importance of this. After what felt like the millionth time, I finally responded with a shoulder shrug and palms up, "Honestly, anyone who wants their greatest life! I want to work with those who want to be worked with! I want to work with people who are ready for transformation!" I was still the Jaded Quitter. I was the Tired Quitter. I was ready to quit coaching because I didn't believe I was ever going to find the people who wanted to make a difference in their lives. I felt pretty defeated, but even after that minor declaration, the Universe could hardly wait to provide me with what I asked for. I got my first referral! A sweet gal that I had done a sample session with referred her brother to me. I was so excited that he was even slightly interested, that I lowered my suggested rate, and we did a month of coaching. It was a start! It was something!

This young man was a politician by day and artist by night. He wanted to work on his career and relationships, and I was more than ready to get digging with him. We spent a month working together, and his life changed dramatically both in that month, and the months following. He ended an unhealthy relationship and got a promotion! He got back into his artwork and restored meaningful relationships that had fallen by the wayside. Watching his life blossom out of our conversations stunned me. It was incredible to get a true taste of the difference this work could make for anyone. I will never forget his acknowledgement of me in our last call. He said, "Whatever your rate is, I hope you never compromise it again. The work we've done is invaluable, and the difference you have made in my life is immeasurable." I was blown away. I had not truly realized my worth yet. I got the effects of coaching and knew exactly how much one should or could charge, but I wasn't relating to myself as a person or coach worthy of asking for those rates. I had collapsed my own self-worth and fear of money with the transformational phenomenon that is coaching. I was debunking the whole point of coaching: discover your greatness, accept it, and unleash it to impact your life and this world. I saw the greatness in this client, but I couldn't see my own just yet.

Over the course of my career, I have coached insurance agents, authors, stay at home moms, and million-dollar business leaders. I have coached dynamic entrepreneurs, and folks who have felt stuck in the same position for decades. My clients' ages range from early twenties to mid-sixties. In attempting to find my market, I have found humanity. I have found that we are all after the basic human needs of feeling loved, heard, known, and understood. When I got that, I knew I could truly coach anyone ready and willing to take on the work. After finding my own worth in this awareness, I was able to connect my rate to myself. I had no doubts in the difference I was making, and my rate seemed like chump change now. I now understand that coaching is an investment in your fullest life. I know that the quality of life my clients desire is just on the other side of asking and going for it! I have watched them start and end relationships, make career transitions or fall in live with the one they have, and reconnect with their inner being and start shining through. My clients become free to double their income and double their fun. They gain access to a life they love because they take ownership of it.

When I have an introductory call to get acquainted with a potential client, I like to get an idea of what is most important to them. Many people's version of their fullest lives involves having great relationships, fulfilling careers, enhanced well-being, and a positive relation-ship with themselves. Knowing that I am equipped to help them create exactly that, empowers me to relate to myself as a professional with a purpose. It brings me to life when folks invest in themselves, and to have the opportunity to walk with them in their journey toward their dreams. So as a life coach, I keep my client base open to anyone looking for their fullest life, no matter how it looks for them. If they are ready to go for it, I am beyond excited to work with them!

I didn't quit coaching, and I have been sure to create a support structure to keep my quitters at bay. I find so much joy in the work I do, that I set myself up to keep going further and further past my comfort zone. This book is the result me finally giving up giving up. It is a result of accepting myself exactly for who I am, and starting my mission with myself. It is a product of understanding and accepting my life purpose. It is a direct result of choosing my life from an empowering place.

I misunderstood the concept of purpose for the first twenty-seven years of my life. I thought purpose showed up in the form of a role, like teacher, coach, or Mom. I thought my purpose was strictly about serving others. Before quitting people pleasing, I related to purpose as martyrdom. I thought my purpose showed up as a job or title, and I certainly wasn't inspired by any of that.

Come to find out, life's purpose shows up as what you are committed to, when all feels right in your world. If you had a blank slate granted to you and nothing that you felt you had to achieve, what cause would be worthy of your life? What I discovered is that my life purpose is adventure!

The younger version of me did not enjoy so much spontaneity and adventure. It may have been an underlying current of my personality, but I was much more wound up about knowing, controlling, and calculating. My inner quitter knew how to win within what it knew, so I was not as interested in the unknown aspects of adventure. I could not guarantee my emotional safety from outside my comfort zone. I was insistent upon planning and being strategic about everything. I thought that controlling everything would get rid of my anxiety.

I operated as though I could control the outcome, and it superficially convinced me that by doing so, I would have nothing to worry about.

For those of you who have also taken the 'control' route, you may have come to discover by now that control is an illusion in which attempting to force outcomes only creates an unrealistic expectation left unfulfilled. We aim for perfection when we create expectations, and inevitably fall short of it. That was how I was trying to start my life coaching practice, and I was always falling short of the perfect expectations I had set myself up against.

So, at the ripe old age of twenty-eight, it was quite a relief to find out that my real life purpose is adventure. It granted me permission to be spontaneous, imperfect, and relaxed. It allowed me to practice letting go of the death grip I had on controlling outcomes. Once I was aware of what would set my soul free, I set out on one mission: adventure.

I began with a girls' trip to the Smokey Mountains. As managers of gyms, we were enforcers of rules, regulations, and policies. We were planners who followed up and followed through. Our work lives were built on a foundation of structure and predictability. When Esme' said, "Hey! You ladies want to spend a weekend in a cabin in Tennessee?" my first move was to go to my packed calendar. I thumbed through three months of weekends already planned. It was a tight squeeze for me because I was still working my way out of my rigid planning lifestyle, and this getaway weekend would be the first attempt at letting go of it. After the five of us worked out our schedules, we packed up her gold Ford Explorer and headed on an exploration. I was still wrapped up in my rigidity going into this trip. I wasn't the one driving, I didn't pick where we were staying, and I had no idea what we would be doing. My inner control freak was not thrilled about this trip in the days leading up to it.

The moment I jumped in the back seat, I decided I was going to practice all the new breakthroughs I felt I was having. I practiced being okay with not knowing and going with someone else's flow. The drive was beautiful and relaxing. We arrived to an insanely awesome, and *giant,* log cabin with a hot tub and a killer view. As the trip went on, I stopped practicing and just started being! I was falling in love with the freedom of enjoying the moment. We drank, we laughed, we danced, and I think we cried, but overall, we had an amazing time. It was exactly what I needed at that time in my life. It truly was an adventure. Because of this trip, I experienced a new place, made new amazing friends, and logged in great new memories!

Upon my arrival back to 'reality,' I became a force to be reckoned with! It was like a point of no return. I got a taste of what it's like to relax on 'figuring it out' and got a chance to just be me. From here, every day became an adventure. Every minute. Every encounter. Every opportunity. I began to see the world through my adventure goggles! For me, living my purpose of adventure meant choosing to really live.

I applied this lesson to my life coaching, and every call was an adventure. I was okay when a sample session didn't end with a new client. Starting journeys with new clients was like taking a trip together, and the thing about an adventure is that no matter how it goes, it is still an adventure. If you decide to go for a hike and fall and break your arm, the experience ensues. It is all a part of the story of the adventure. Walking away from the nine-to-five and into entrepreneurship with no guarantees was a great adventure. It was scary. It was uncertain. I had my doubts, but I made it an adventure the entire way.

The more often I packed up and headed out, the more exciting my adventure became. Enjoying this earth for the time that I occupy it has become my greatest 'job.' I create as much fun in life as humanly possible. I choose to live in the present moment minute to minute, day to day, to week, to month, to year. To simply enjoy the life that I have has become an amazing journey. Along the way, I have met new mates. I have encountered more opportunities. I stopped waiting and worrying, and walked out into the world of possibility. As a result, fellow travelers have crossed my path that have enriched my life, and I, theirs. I am seeing more of this world every day and who I get to be in it.

Accepting my life purpose has me living with a fiery passion. I am on this earth to help heal and inspire others. Whether it's by the one or by the thousands, I am here to live by and set the example that you can live the life you love, by simply living as yourself. There's no one to be but you, and there's nothing to do but be. The conversations I was having about how many clients I had on my payroll faded. Being a walking, talking example of this work became my priority. I came to know and trust that I would attract the people seeking their fullest lives, and our work together would become clear. Attracting this client base has become second nature for me, and I have enjoyed walking side by side with people on their journeys to having their dreams fulfilled.

You can never un-become yourself. You can never quit on the soul that resides within your skin. Your energy will always be bursting at the seams. Accept that undying passion and celebrate that energy. Your purpose exists in that constant gravitational pull toward what moves you. When you accept it for exactly what it is; your purpose, you will become a beacon of light. You will experience a life worth living, a career worth having, and a purpose worth calling your own. You may find yourself living from an empowered place, and you may find yourself living a life you love.

Reflection Questions:

What are the limiting beliefs or insecurities that you have about yourself?

How are they holding you back?

If you let go of the need to control, in what ways would you become free?

If you truly had a blank slate, what cause would be worthy of your life?

If you can sense your purpose, what is in the way of you living it on purpose?

Do you believe that you have the potential to create a powerful, thriving life out of your passion and natural talents? What about that potential scares the bejesus out of you?
What would it look like for you to be a walking, talking, living, and breathing example of pure love in this world?

If you set your soul free, where would it take you?

Chapter 6

Commitment

I once observed a man admit that he was committed to maintaining his weight. Doctors and family had told him that he was overweight, but he confessed that he was not concerned about it. For years, he pretended to be working on it, while behind closed doors, he was not. He agreed to go home and share this open admission with his family. For him to own his weight and end the charade set him free from maintaining this facade with his wife and children. I saw him the next day with his wife, holding hands as she leaned onto him lovingly. They were laughing and being playful, and they were absolutely beaming. This man had finally committed to living out loud and it was apparent. He owned his personal commitment, his body, and himself, and it was obvious, he had set himself free. His wife seemed to be overjoyed just to have her husband being authentic with her. It was apparent that they were on the same page and it was heartwarming. It seemed to have saved a dying relationship.

At first, seeing this example of commitment really twisted up my mind. Raised as a non-quitter, I only understood commitment to mean relentless hard work. It meant showing up to everything you were told to do, and doing everything to the best of your ability. Being from the Midwest, I wore commitment like I wore my blue collar: proudly. In my eyes, to be committed meant that I had a strong character and superior ability to persevere. I relied on it throughout my life. I led group projects in school, and took every leadership role I saw available. I was the most committed person I knew, or so I thought.

To see this man display commitment in a completely new way distorted my limited view of what I understood it to be. Through a ton of life coaching practice, I built a new relationship to this concept. I got to see that EVERYONE is always committed...always. What I had not understood was the difference in what we are committed to. In school, I was committed to being the best and took on all sorts of responsibility. When others weren't aligned with my priorities, I made it mean they didn't have any. I translated it to mean that they weren't committed people. To find out that we simply weren't committed to the same things in life had me meeting EVERYONE so differently. I gained a new appreciation for people. I couldn't wait to start finding out what others were striving for to and it had me seeing variety, excitement, and possibility in all of them. I gained the insight that set me free from my struggles with commitment. I was able to align with others who shared my same priorities. This made work, play, and life much more enjoyable. The rift I had created by trying to make things work simply dissipated, and I saw myself walking in the same direction of the people I was involved with. I became empowered to facilitate a conversation that would move everyone toward clarity, and make group choices that left everyone walking away with a win. Rebuilding my relationship to commitment has been a true gift to my life.

I went skydiving for the first time in San Diego one summer. It was one of those 'life peak' moments in which everything you have been dwelling on just clicks. It was a moment in which I truly understood living for commitments that leave me feeling enlivened and fulfilled...*really* enlivened in this example.

I was the last one to board the plane, which meant I was the first to jump. This had not occurred to me as we boarded but it certainly became obvious when we all turned to prep for departure. I got a rush of "WE'RE DOIN' IT!" I got the excitement jitters and that sort of "oh, shit!" fear about how this was about to go down. Strapped to the front of him like a baby koala, my tandem pro jumper and I stepped to the wide-open door of the plane.

While prepping on the ground, the instructors had

taught us the 'banana technique' in which we backwards wrap our bodies around our pros and let them lead the jump. So, as we simply leaned backward out of a moving plane at ten thousand feet, my inner critic was screaming "BANANA! BANANA! BANANA!!!" What I was really saying to myself was "Do it right! Don't screw it up!" the phrase my inner quitter has operated from her whole life.

Within seven seconds of leaving the plane, I let my life coach training guide the experience. I silenced my inner beatings, acknowledged that I am skydiving with a professional jumper, let go of the need to control, and committed to enjoying the experience and the views. As I continued to fall, my inner dialogue shifted: "I am free falling. I have jumped off a plane and I am free falling into a life that I love! The sun is shining and the winds are whipping and the world beneath me is turning! I have an aerial view of my circumstances and I am being who I want to be, despite any of them! I have jumped off a plane and am diving headfirst into commitment! I am dedicated to the fullest life I can create and I am creating it! I AM DOING IT! Holy shit, I am really doing it!"

I jumped off that plane and really understood how free I am. I am free to be me. I am free to live out loud. I am free to be grateful, free to love and be loved, free to be all of it and have it all. The key to having it all is deciding that you already do. In that moment I decided. I am free to fall and I am free to fly. I choose to fly.

My commitments became crystal clear. Just as

discussed earlier in this book, our happiness does not exist in our futures. My commitments are not something to be put 'out there' for 'someday,' they are to be lived from every day, every breath, in every way.

In the light of watching that man admit to sticking with his weight, I had been pondering what in life was I committed to that I wasn't admitting. The commitments I have consciously chosen to live by are to be a positive impact in the world and an advocate in ontology. I am dedicated to living *on* purpose and *with* purpose. I pledge to creating life as an adventure every day. This last one took some learning, but I have resolved that I will not consider others' decisions as 'wrong,' but instead recognize the differences in priorities. As a learned life coach, my ultimate commitment in and out of 'work' is that I am undyingly devoted to unleashing as many hearts as I possibly can.

I have chosen purposeful commitments that create an experience of full freedom, power, and self-expression. I don't work a day in my life. I live. I live in such a way that generates energy, vitality, and excitement. Even the 'stuff' of life that may seem burdensome looks different from this perspective. The 'stuff' becomes an opportunity to expand the capacity of how we handle life.

We are all committed but it is vital to uncover in what ways you are, personally. We are all often drawn to some version of being comfortable. We generate a sense of predictability in order to feel like we can relax about what the future may bring. We create a routine and even if it is lackluster, at least we know what to expect. This can become disappointing over years and decades due to the same, predictable patterns playing out. The same can apply to romantic relationships, and reasonably, we end up constantly finding ourselves wanting more. Let's not forget the fact that it can really turn us upside down if life doesn't go according to plan.

The funny thing about commitment is that it is freeing! We believe that instead, it puts us in a restrictive bubble that limits who and what we can be. Alternatively, commitment sets us free to be ourselves so shamelessly that we then get to choose who we are! Similar to the man who owned his weight, finding out what you are committed to and simply being openly committed to it shall set you free. I invite you to take a look at your commitments in an honest way. To finally see, and acknowledge that you are committed to staying safe, for example, will turn it into an intentional, powerful choice. To see that certain commitments of yours may be holding you back from feeling alive may inspire you to choose new ones. Either way, you are taking your power back and can begin generating your life, as opposed to being a victim of it.

As stated in various ways throughout this book, life doesn't happen to you. You happen to life. You happen to this world. You happen to the people you encounter. You happen. You matter. You make a difference. You choose what difference that is.

I invite you to make choices that bring you to
life every day, and to follow your heart.

I invite you to choose commitments that have you
jumping out of bed to deliver your gift to the world.

I will always invite you to live a life you love.

Acknowledgements

To my parents, you deserve your operator's license for running this roller coaster for the last twenty-eight years. You keep me on track and maintain my bearings to keep going day after day. From a joy ride to a thrilling eighty-foot drop, I know you're always up for the twists and turns. I owe you my life and to honor that, I promise to always live it to the fullest until the very last ride.

I would like to use this book as an opportunity to make a formal apology to my college teammates, coaches, and trainers. I would like to take responsibility for the impact that my personal suffering had on the team. I would love to thank and acknowledge you for graciously accepting me and loving me through the toughest time of my life. For you, I am ever grateful.

To my sister, to my forever neighbor; near or far, you are always 'next door' to my heart. You, my dearest, are a spark for my soul. Your trailblazing ways have inspired me every single day. I know I can do anything because you have already done tried it. "Proud" doesn't serve justice to how I feel about being your big sis but if you can believe it, I am at a loss for words. You are everything, Emily Ann.

To the wackiest bunch of coconuts I'll ever know, my family and best friend, I LOVE YOU! You are my launching pad, parachute, and crash pad in life. I can do anything with y'all in my corner. THANK YOU for you endless love, support, and guidance. I am beyond proud to be born of this blood and being from the Little City by the Lake.

To the community that raised me, from those moms (and dads) that did love me as their own to the friends who granted me grace in my growth. My bond with my hometown grows stronger and stronger. There is a wholeness about our beautiful city filled with love, heart, celebration, belonging, and possibility. There is a unique, homemade and hand-delivered goodness about what lies within our city limits. It is a village...of lovers, family, and friends that have truly raised one another. Thank you for being a community I can count on. Whiting is, and always will be my home ♥

I am who I am because of the women who raised me. In this Tribe, one may slip, but no one gets left behind. You ladies are power, courage, heart, grace, and light in this world.

I would like to express my undying love for my Father, the man who taught me how to love and be loved with my whole heart. "Abigail Rose, gentle as a lamb, tough as a boy. To all a friend, to her father, a joy"

It is from the deepest, most grateful part of my heart that I thank you for reading this book! It is my intention to share the possibility of transformation with the world. Whether it be by the one or one thousand, it is my driving passion to touch and unleash as many as I can in this life that I am given.

Thank you for being one of those hearts. I invite you to join me in my 'save the world' mission & request that you share this book and be responsible for unleashing the heart! You are gift in this world. Your impact is irreplicable.

Be you, do you, have the life you love

Abigail

About the Author

Liver of life and lover of love, Abigail Gazda has transformed her passion for education into a full-time career. As a life coach, author, and motivational speaker, she empowers clients and hosts group events around the country. The transformative work she does invites people to take a much closer look at who they are being, in order to shift the relationship to the circumstances they have generated. As an advocate of ontology, she helps others accept that they are perfect, whole, and complete.

Through her Instagram account (_Instagail_) and blog (AbigailGazda.com) she promotes introspective reflection and shines a light on what there is to be grateful for in this world.

Abigail loves to share her breakthroughs in her writing as evidence of what is available to anyone with a commitment to their fullest life.

With a kind smile and full heart, Gazda loves to love and support others in cultivating their own self-love.

As described in her book, *Giving Up Giving Up: The Memoir of a Quitter*, she is on a 'save the world' mission to unleash the hearts of this world to create a positive impact of connection, authenticity, and passion. She lives to adventure this world spreading love, kindness, and joy.

Born and raised a proud Indiana Hoosier, Abigail now resides in Southern California.

Gazda hosts group coaching events around the country. She creates the space for participants to show up authentically and transparently in order to get the breakthroughs they come for. Group event conversations vary from personal or relationship to well-being, career, and beyond. To attend an event or book Abigail in your area, visit abigailgazda.com to co-create new possibility!